John Hartig   Two B

Two Baroque Prodigies
Quantz and Leclair
Flute and Violin

Design and Writing
John Hartig
Copyright © 2022
Revised Edition 2024

Published on Amazon and Kindle
with thanks for the chance
to publish affordably
and for the helpful phone chats

John Hartig

Dedication

These short stories are dedicated to all the unknown authors who have not made a name for themselves but who keep writing and publishing anyway because of an inner need. These two novellas ae based on true stories with, of course, a liberal sprinkling of my imagination.

I hope you enjoy my take on the biographies of these two great Baroque virtuosi: Book 1 on Johann Joachim Quantz, who excelled in the flute and Book 2 on Jean-Marie Leclair, who challenged his peers to violin "duels".

History and Background

Two of the Greats
Johann Joachim Quantz 1697-1773
Jean-Marie Leclair 1697-1764

"The Baroque Era of Music" refers to Western classical music composed from 1600 to 1750. This era followed the Renaissance and was followed in turn by the Classical period. The Baroque Era embraced such notable names as Johann Sebastian Bach, his son C.P.E. Bach, George Frideric Handel, Antonio Vivaldi, Claudio Monteverdi and Alessandro Scarlatti.

The term "baroque" comes from the Portuguese word, *barroco*, which means "misshapen pearl". During this period, composers experimented with finding a fuller sound for each instrument, thus creating "the orchestra".

*****

There are 3 sub-divisions to the Baroque Era.

Early Baroque from 1580-1650, for example the works of Claudio Monteverdi. The Middle Baroque from 1630-1700, during the Age of Absolutism personified in Louis XIV reign of France. The demand for chamber music increased. An example of a court style composer was Jean Baptiste Lully.

The middle Baroque period had the emergence of the vocal styles of cantata oratorio and opera during the 1630s. Arcangelo Corelli was significant as a violinist who promoted violin technique and advocated the concerto grosso.

The late Baroque period from 1680-1750 saw the works of George Frideric Handel and Johann Sebastian Bach come to the fore. Also, the works of the two Scarlatti, Vivaldi, Rameau and Telemann.

*****

Our two Baroque prodigies stand out as exceptional, although somewhat obscure in history. They were the flute prodigy, Johann Joachim Quantz, 1697-1773, and the multi-talented ballet dancer and violinist, Jean-Marie Leclair, 1697-1764.

It's a shame that most people do not know about them. The passage of time has shuffled them off into obscurity, and they deserve to come forward again, so that they may be known and that their music be enjoyed.

*****

Johann Joachim Quantz's father was a blacksmith. In those days, a boy would follow in his father's profession. Unlike his dad, young Quantz wanted to become a musician. When the father died, before Quantz was 11 years old, the young boy was taken in by musical relatives. He learned all sorts of instruments, notably the flute.

Quantz is known as the private tutor of King Frederick the Great of Prussia, teaching him to play the flute in the King's private chamber group. Quantz stayed in the King's employ in Berlin until Quantz died in 1773 at the age of 76.

Jean-Marie Leclair was born to a family who were milliners. Leclair became a superb ballet dancer and violinist. In fact, he excelled on the violin to become a virtuoso competing in violin "duels" with the likes of

Locatelli. Leclair played first chair in King Louis XV's orchestra of France.

Leclair, however, was murdered, stabbed in the back on his way home one night in Paris. He was 67 years old. No one was ever arrested for the crime! It remained a mystery as to who actually killed him!

I got the idea for writing a Baroque murder mystery from a little anecdote I heard on The Oasis, a radio show on Toronto's radio station, Classical 96.3 FM.

A violinist, murdered? Nobody knows "who dunnit"? Why not solve It? So, my disclaimer in this story is my fertile imagination. Who's to prove me wrong? Only history knows the truth!

John Hartig,
Canadian author

BOOK 1
Johann Joachim Quantz
Forword

Johann Joachim Quantz did not have the makings of a blacksmith like his father. He was born skinny and frail in 1697. His father, Andreas, was disappointed in the fragile little bundle which was presented to him as his son. He had hoped for something more robust.

It was fortunate, in a way, that Andreas, the father, died, shy of his son's 11th birthday. Young Johann was destined for something better anyway, more than what a dark and grimy blacksmith shop could give him. Had he assumed his father's trade, he might have been called by his birth name, Hanss [a familiar rendition of Johann], but since his Uncle Justus Quantz took him in, the little boy's destiny would shine brightly in the annals of flute playing, as "Johann Joachim Quantz". He was one of the greatest flautists of the Baroque Era during the 18th century! He added two new keys to the flute and perfected its intonation.

*****

My research on Johann Joachim Quantz yielded about 35 pages of a biography with interesting dates and tidbits on the man. Not enough for a full and deserving book on him! I had to come up with a plan to stretch my writings out to get an enjoyable short story out of it. So, I plugged in the spark of my imagination.

I acknowledge taking license, in mixing the facts with fiction on how things might have transpired in certain parts of the man's private life.

Quantz never really revealed anything about his private life anyway in his autobiography, which was written as a "prim and proper" account, listing all his laudable achievements, his promotions and his increase in salaries. The autobiography was published in 1755 by Friedrich Wilhelm Marpurg. There was also a continuation in 1762 for Padre Martini. *[source: Feike Bonnema website 2016]*

*****

Johann Joachim Quantz' life can be divided into four sections: his youth, life in Dresden, his tour of Europe, and his life in Berlin.

I make no claim to accuracy in all details in my book, since I said, my book was stretched out with my imagination to facilitate little anecdotes as fillers to make the book an enjoyable read. However, most of the dates and the run of the man's life are correct.

Quantz set an example when he wrote his "*Versuch* or *Attempt*" in how to play the flute, published in German and French in 1752. Carl Philipp Emmanuel Bach published something similar on how to play the keyboard in 1755 and Agricola followed, in 1757, with his proper method of singing.

It is hoped that the reader will be able to tell when my book goes into flights of fancy and that the reader will appreciate my fabricated little additions. Therefore, there is detailed historical information in my book, as well as imaginative fiction to make this little volume a pleasure to read.

John Hartig,
Vineland author

1
Changed Destiny

Johann Joachim Quantz

Perhaps, people make their own destinies. They have so much to work against, their time in history, their station, their parents and their health. As mentioned, Hanss Jochim Quantz was born a scrawny little thing in 1697. His father could not picture this puny bundle ever becoming a blacksmith. How could he take over Andreas' shop which required massive muscles and the sweat of the brow!

It is ironic that France's virtuoso violinist, Jean-Marie Leclair, was born in the same year, 1697. Whereas Leclair came from a family of clothes makers who had a penchant for the arts, like dancing and music, Quantz' family came from the lower working-class with a father who wielded a heavy hammer in a blacksmith shop.

Hanss was born in the village of Oberscheden in the province of Hanover in Northwestern Germany. It was a cold snowy January when Hanss was born. Nothing seemed warm or propitious about the boy's birth.

His mother, Anna Ilse, died in 1702 when Quantz was only 5. The father, Andreas, did the best he could. He remarried a year later because his 5 kids needed a mother. During those times, things were done out of necessity. Love and the fine arts were luxuries. Andreas' new wife had to come into the household as a cook and do the domestic chores for the family of 5 kids.

The father, Andreas, showed the boy how to operate the bellows, but little Hanss was so small that it was doubtful he would ever have the stature to be a "man" who could wield such an apparatus. His father smiled indulgently when he saw his son struggle to pump the big bellows which heated the forge. "He's just a child," he told himself, "Maybe he'll grow into it?"

Andreas used the boy as a "go-fer" to fetch nails and horseshoes after school. Hanss didn't especially like the work in the shop. He did like school though, learning his numbers and letters easily in the *Grundschule* or elementary school, until he was 9 years old. That was the extent of most boys' education in those days when the parents could not afford higher education. By the time a boy was 10, he was eligible to be apprenticed in a trade.

His father was actually glad when Hanss finished his rudimentary education. Up to that point, Andreas had to appeal to the principal to protect his boy from the bullies in school who felt that a skinny weakling was an easy target. They pushed him around during the morning break or whenever the teacher was not looking, giving him a quick smack on the back of the head.

Hanss had small shoulders and spindly legs. "Look at the blacksmith's son," his classmates taunted. "He throws the ball like a girl." They also made up a cruel, dirty little rhyme with his name: "Quantz, Quantz mit dem langen Schwantz!" [Quantz, Quantz with the big, long wang]. The teacher took on the task of guardian because Hanss was a decent boy who enjoyed learning, unlike some of the cruder children in the village.

Hanss often cried himself to sleep at night. However, he fell asleep knowing that there was something special about him. "Dear God," he prayed, "let me grow up into something useful."

Hanss had already shown his interest in music when he accompanied his eldest brother, Jost Matthies on the double bass at the age of 8, when his brother played for the dance music in village festivals. At this time, Hanss did the accompaniment on the double bass without being able to read a note. *[source: Kayla Ann Low dissertation p.10]*

Andreas persisted in his son becoming a blacksmith. In fact, he pleaded with the boy even on his deathbed, to follow in his destined footsteps. Hanss wasn't quite 11 yet. To please his father, the boy replied submissively, "Yes, Papa."

In 1707, both the father and stepmother died. Hanss and his four siblings were orphans. Where would they go? What would they do?

Relatives decided to disperse them and gave them a choice as to which relatives would be their guardians. The children chose according to the type of apprenticeship they could have. Hanss already knew. He chose Uncle Justus who was the town musician in Merseburg.

Uncle Justus talked it over with his wife. "He is such a little boy. Not much of a mouth to feed. Let's take him in. The boy doesn't look like a blacksmith anyway; maybe we can make a musician out of him?"

Hanss was happy when he heard that Uncle Justus would take him in. His hopes and dreams were to become a musician anyway, not a blacksmith, despite the promise to his dying father.

Unfortunately, three months into his new home, the uncle also passed away. However, Justus' son-in-law, Johann Adolf Fleischhack, took over for care of the boy. He said, "If you are going to be a musician, we have to get rid of that boyish name, 'Hanss'. We will call you Johann Joachim Quantz from now on. Now, that name has a ring of respectability to it."

2
Next Guardian

In his autobiography, Quantz describes Fleischhack as an "inattentive teacher". He did not always provide the best musical training for his students. [Ref: Kayla Ann Low, Master of Music thesis, 2022, Lost in Translation, p.11]

Johann Joachim Quantz improved in health, and with his health, he also improved in height. By the time he was 17 or 18, he grew several inches to a respectable height in those days at 5'8" tall. His bones also thickened up so that his father, had he lived, would have been proud of him, despite not becoming a blacksmith! Quantz was less likely to be picked on by the bullies of the world.

On the other hand, Frederick the Great was also a small boy, but stayed small becoming a small man at 5'3". But then, he had the tall advantage of being the monarch!

This is so unlike the tall actor who portrayed the monarch in the 1984 film *Amadeus*. So, much for artistic license. Forgive me then, for letting my fancy run free from time to time in this book.

Johann Joachim Quantz stayed with Adolf Fleischhack for 5 years as an apprentice and two years as a journeyman. Quantz learned an array of musical instruments because a town musician was expected to be versatile in every instrument. He also took on the keyboard with the Merseburg organist, Johann Friedrich Kiesewetter. In his autobiography Quantz said: *'It is in Dresden or Berlin that, in time, I would like to take up residence because I think I would hear more beautiful music there and be able to learn more than in Merseburg.' [naxos.com, J.J. Quantz]*

*****

Johann Joachim Quantz was a poly-instrumental prodigy, becoming proficient not only in one, but several instruments. A town musician must be proficient in everything musical, so Quantz did just that! He learned the violin, oboe, trumpet, cornett, trombone, horn, recorder, bassoon, cello, viola da gamba and the double bass! *[Feike Bonnema website, 2016]*

The flute, meanwhile, waited in the wings as a distant destiny. As one reads Quantz' autobiography, one can't help but notice the lack of modesty. Quantz says right out, he has talent! He's not shy about it, but he also says, he worked hard!

> I wanted to be nothing but a musician…The first instrument which I had to learn was the violin, for which I also seemed to have the greatest ability. Thereon, followed the oboe and the trumpet. During my years as an apprentice, I worked the hardest on these three instruments. *[Autobiog. 1755]*

The violin was his favourite instrument. By the age of 16, in December 1713, he was already able to play works by Corelli and Telemann. He was making a name for himself, and he was gainfully employed by the town of Radeberg as an up-and-coming town musician. But that only lasted three weeks! Quantz' position as town piper went up in smoke when Radeberg burned down to the ground after a lightning strike.

John Hartig   Two Baroque Prodigies

It's strange how tragedies work out for the best sometimes, in this case the advancement of Quantz' career. He moved to Pirna the day after the fire. He became town piper there in 1714. He was only 17 years of age!

It was in Pirna where young Quantz got to see the sheet music for Vivaldi's *Violin Concertos* for the first time. He was impressed. He took further training in all his instruments, which meant, violin, oboe, trumpet, cornett, French horn, trombone, recorder, bassoon, cello, viol and double bass! The flute was not far off! Quantz's talents and ambitions were bursting at the seams; he was outgrowing a little town. He wanted more than what Pirna could give him.

Pirna was close to Dresden. In Pirna, Quantz got to know the Dresden town band director, Gottfried Heine, who hired him when he needed extras to play at weddings, sometimes in Dresden, a musical center. *[Kayla Ann Low dissertation p.12]*

Dresden and Berlin were key cities for musical talent, and young Johann Joachim Quantz hoped to get a position somewhere within one of them. He wanted to leave memories of little towns like Merseburg, Radeberg and Pirna behind. The big cities of Europe beckoned him. He set his sights first on Dresden. Why should he not have fame, make good money, and create superb music?

3
Fleischhack

Of course, there was so much that Quantz had to overcome in his station, and as well, in his location. Some of it, of course, seemed to be luck. In a way, it was lucky his father had died. Uncle Justus took him in. Then Uncle Justus' son in law also took him in. Although the boy had a roof over his head, the young Quantz had to deal with his new guardian, Johann Adolf Fleischhack, as an "inattentive" teacher which stood in the way of Quantz' musical development. *[Kayla Ann Low dissertation p.12]*

One can only guess as to why Fleischhack was inattentive. Certainly, little Quantz was not a direct part of the family! But at least, he was fed and clothed. As a result, Quantz was left to fend for himself most days, do errands and learn music, basically, on his own. He had all the formal education he was ever going to get, so he had his basic numbers and letters. If he had no inner drive, he would never have amounted to anything. No flute, no Quantz! But, the young man did have this inner drive, and above all a talent and intelligence that superseded Fleischhack.

Furthermore, the latent genetic inheritance from his father finally kicked in, giving him a tall stature for those days, at 5'8" with broad shoulders. Quantz became stronger and taller physically after his puny start when he was 10. Fleischhack, in fact, remarked, "When you came to us, you were a weakling, young Quantz, but now look at you. You are growing like a weed. Maybe, you will have to work twice as hard before you eat us out of house and home!"

Quantz made it his business to go to the homes of various musicians in the town to learn how to play anything from the violin to the double bass. Up to that point, he had merely improvised by ear when he played the double bass at weddings.

As young Quantz grew taller and stronger, his confidence grew too. In fact, he wore a certain air of arrogance about himself as a coat of armour against those who used to pick on him and those who thought they were better than he was.

One of the older boys in the town's musicians' group made a cruel remark about the orphan boy one day, about the boy who had no parents. Quantz grabbed him by the lapel and gave him a bloody nose. Fleischhack, when he heard about the incident, was not too happy about it. He had to do some diplomatic talking to smooth things over with the other boy's parents.

Then at home, Fleischhack had a few things to say to Quantz who had become a strapping lad at 15.

"Quantz," he said, "listen to me. You must protect your fingers. Don't injure them by getting into senseless fights. They are our livelihood. If somebody insults you, it's better to swallow the remark, than to lose your ability to play music. Do you understand?"

The boy listened submissively and said, "Yes sir." He took his guardian's advice to heart.

Quantz continued to grow and stayed out of fights. He became proficient in all manner of instruments mostly through his own initiative and persistence to get free lessons from those who enjoyed seeing Quantz's eagerness to learn something new. Quantz took care of his fingers and was grateful that he was blessed with a keen memory and an accurate ear for pitch.

Quantz hated being an orphan. It was that fear of being alone which sparked his urge to become independent and better than his peers. He quickly learned the violin, oboe, trumpet, cornett, trombone, horn, recorder, bassoon, cello, viola da gamba, followed by the oboe, and trumpet. He worked the hardest on the oboe, trumpet and violin, preferring the violin over the rest of his impressive roster.

*****

Quantz needed no incentive from Fleischhack during this apprenticeship. Fleischhack basically let Quantz run his own education because the boy obviously knew what he was doing where music was concerned. Quantz was so independent that he learned composition on his own. He assiduously studied the works of Telemann, Melchior Hofmann, and Johann David Heinich during his harpsichord studies with the help of a relative named Johann Friedrich Kiesewetter.

Kiesewetter was more engaging than Fleischhack in teaching young Quantz music. Quantz acknowledges in his autobiography, "through his instruction I laid the first groundwork for understanding harmony, and probably first received the desire to learn composition." *[Kayla Ann Low dissertation, p.12]*

By the end of his apprenticeship with Fleischhack, Quantz had turned into a self-confident young man. Some of the older musicians in town thought he had become a young peacock, however.

Fleischhack drew him aside one day and advised him, "Quantz, you will be leaving my nest soon. I advise you not to parade your talent so openly in front of your peers. You could make enemies that way." Quantz was too young to appreciate that remark. After all, he had worked hard for his skills and played better than any other town musician in the band. He knew that he would leave Pina soon and that Dresden was calling him. He was ready to go.

4
Jealousies

While still a teenager, the other town musicians treated the young man civilly, except on a few occasions when jealousy reared its ugly head where egos were concerned. Quantz got along quite well with his Conductor, with the Concertmaster and the more proficient musicians. But with the less able and the older musicians, who thought they had "seniority", he had a problem. They were set in their ways. To see a mere boy, play better than they, rubbed them the wrong way.

They were used to the pecking order and occasionally muttered under their breath insulting things about the young man, who in their eyes seemed rather haughty. They resisted his authority because he was, after all, a young peacock, too flashy and smart for his own good.

The boy not only played the most difficult notes in a piece precisely, but he imbued those notes with a lovely lyricism.

As mentioned, Johann Joachim Quantz became proficient in the violin, trumpet and a roster of other instruments, playing them better than his colleagues in the band. Afterwards he added the flute and even the piano to his skills, he became a very marketable commodity. The nobility within the European courts noticed his playing at various events.

Quantz seemed to inhale music. He was like a sponge when it came to understanding and playing melodies.

John Hartig   Two Baroque Prodigies

Johann Joachim Quantz was blessed with perfect pitch and an eidetic memory.

In his early career, he started out as an oboist. He was so good that he was appointed, as oboist to the court of Augustus II, King of Poland and Elector of Saxony. Quantz was a mere 21 years of age!

In 1724, when he was 27, he noticed that there were too many good oboists to compete with. He wondered which other instrument was more marketable.

The average musician would have been content to be stuck on the same rung. He could have been happy in his "station" to live in a little town, giving private flute lessons to mediocre students for the rest of his life. It would have been a satisfactory living.

*****

Instead, Quantz cut a new path for himself, concentrating on the flute, on which, within a few years, he was considered one of the finest in all of Europe!

When his Conductor or Concertmaster invited Quantz to lunch, it was a "working lunch" to talk about the program, the repertoire and how to seat musicians so that the band would create the most harmonious sound. Quantz had the responsibility, as well, of transcribing music for other instruments and making sure everyone had their sheets before a performance started. He was reliable.

He displayed confidence which came across as a kind of arrogance. But then, if you are so talented, maybe people mistake confidence for arrogance.

This did not always sit well with older musicians who were relegated to the back rows because they played music in the old style, note for note. When the Conductor asked Quantz to sit up front, one senior at the back remarked quietly and snidely, "He knows how to network!" And indeed, he did, not in a deliberate self-serving manner, but as a by-product of his gregarious spirit and his natural talent. He loved talking musical ideas and feelings with people who understood those things on a higher level.

John Hartig   Two Baroque Prodigies

5
Appearances

There are two paintings which show that Quantz had become stockier in later years. Perhaps, he might have met his father's standards after all as a blacksmith, but then, that would have been a waste of his talent and deprived the world of many fine musical pieces for the flute.

The Royal Academy of Music has a painting by an unknown artist, showing Quantz giving Frederick a lesson on the flute. The figures are sitting side by side. It is clear who is the stockier figure. Quantz, on the left, is wearing the traditional tricorne hat of those days. Frederick is the skinny figure on the right, hunched over in his red coat. It's been said that His Majesty was about 5'3" tall.

Adolph Menzel painted a lovely portrait in 1852 of a concert given by Frederick the Great in the decorated hall of his castle, *Sanssouci*, [meaning, "without worry"]. This painting was of course done 100 years after it happened. One can only hope Menzel got his proportions and his heights right in the portrait.

C.P.E. Bach is seated at the harpsichord, while His Majesty is at the center of the picture giving the concert on the flute. Quantz is at the far right leaning against the wall, a tall figure.

It is clear that His Majesty is diminutive with fine features and skinny legs. Quantz, on the other hand, even leaning against the wall, comes across as a larger person with a stockier frame. Quantz looks like he is the same height as His Majesty though, but then, we must remember that Quantz is leaning back against the wall. Quantz could, therefore, be taken to be between 5'6" to 5'8" tall.

Charles Burney met Quantz when the man was 75 years old. He recalls that the veteran musician was "of an uncommon size", with broad shoulders and gigantic limbs. He had the build of a blacksmith; his father would indeed have been proud. He exhibited health and vigour for a person of that age. Therefore, for those days, some 250 years ago, Quantz being on the high side of 5'8" tall seems indeed, as Burney described him, "of an uncommon size".

I checked the proportions of the figures in Menzel's painting in a photographic program called *Fireworks* with the Grid display on. I know the portrait was painted a century after such a performance occurred, but one must trust the accurate depiction of the painter. Quantz was at least of regular height, whereas Frederick the Great was a small man, unlike the actors who played him in modern movies.

There is a verbal description of Quantz cited in Feike Bonnema's website, in the Quote portion where Carl Phillipp Emanuel Bach comments: "He [Quantz] is described as tall and stout in person, grave in disposition and rough in manners."

Being a blacksmith's son, one can accept Quantz as having rough manners, but to be "grave in disposition", is hard to accept. He must have been liked by many at court because he was a man who even loved a joke or two. To rub shoulders with high society, we must give Quantz credit for his tall talent and his ability to chat intelligently with his betters, which was his ticket to upper mobility in Baroque society.

*****

On the more serious side, Quantz was not only gifted, but he was a disciplined and hard-working person, mastering intonation and smooth timing in his music. He did not take his talent for granted and worked hard through his God-given gift. Yes, his fellow musicians were jealous, although Quantz did not deliberately make them so.

Wilhelmine von Bayreuth wrote to her brother Frederick about how her own flute lessons were going, noting that Quantz was "obedient as a lamb". She also surmised that jealousy must have been involved when Quantz taught Frederick at Ruppin, "because presumably it annoyed Quantz that you play as well as he does." *[Excerpt from a 1736 letter of Wilhelmine to her brother, Frederick, cited by Feike Bonnema]*

I suspect though that Quantz' station in life in those days might have involved a little chicanery in his part, as to how excellent the Emperor really played because after all the Emperor was the Emperor and Quantz knew how to play the game of social status.

Presumably, Quantz was just flattering His Majesty the King, by saying that Frederick was as good a player as he was. That's the way things were done in those days in terms of social courtesies. Flattery was a way for a servant, even a servant considered as a friend, to remain in the King's graces. If His Majesty was every bit as good as Quantz on the flute, why would His Majesty ever have continued taking lessons from the maestro?

*****

Quantz' life seemed to be one of "two steps back and one giant leap forward". From the age of 16 on, he was eager to get permanent work. However, it seemed like fate sabotaged his hopes.

Prince Friedrich Erdmann, the brother of the Duke of Merseburg, died. A three-month moratorium on music was declared! After the mourning period ["Landestrauer"] ended, Quantz performed in Merseburg and was obviously noticed for his captivating playing style.

Pirna had been good for him. He was declared town piper quite quickly by June 1714. The promotion and also the close location to Dresden also had given him more opportunity to be noticed. And noticed he was, because he played the flute like no one else in Europe! Dresden was the next move!

6
Dresden

Johann Joachim Quantz was invited to join the Stadtkapelle, the city's chapel in Dresden, by Gottfried Hayne who had been the Crown Prince's childhood music teacher. In 1716, Quantz was 19 years of age. He finally made the big move to Dresden, a center for the Arts.

In March 1716, he got a job in the Stadtkapelle for Dresden playing oboe and flute. He stayed in that service for two years and then became oboist at the Polish Orchestra of Augustus II, accompanying the King to Poland on a regular basis.

Quantz was restless and ambitious. He was not content to be just a musician content to stay in one place and be happy giving lessons to the well-to-do for the rest of his life. Instead, he took lessons in Vienna in 1717 in counterpoint from renowned people like Jan Dismas Zelenka and Johann Joseph Fux.

In 1718, Johann Joachim Quantz was 21 years old. As previously mentioned, he became an oboist in the Polish Chapel at the court of Elector August II in Dresden. There were other excellent oboists at the court. No chance for advancement for a young upstart. So, Quantz did an about-face and learned to play the flute instead! He took lessons for a four-month period from Pierre-Gabriel Buffardin, the renowned French flutist in the Dresden court orchestra. Quantz was learning new things all the time and he was also networking with top musicians.

Quantz writes in his autobiography, "the previous flautist, Friese, who had no great inclination toward music, willingly allowed me to take the chair of the first flautist". *[Kayla Ann Low dissertation p.14]*

That's when Quantz started to compose music for the flute because of the paucity of the repertoire for that lovely instrument. Ironically, it was a violinist, Johann Georg Pisendel, a close friend, who encouraged Quantz to write music for the flute which was sorely lacking up that point. Pisendel was the concertmaster for the Royal Orchestra. He challenged Quantz, "If there is no repertoire available for the flute, then create it!"

Quantz did just that! Quantz had the great fortune of being surrounded by the influences of French and Italian styles of music in Dresden. He assimilated these styles like a sponge.

*****

He got to meet several illustrious names of the time who were members of the royal orchestra in Dresden. Quantz liked meeting such high-quality people because these musicians demanded exacting standards, more than "merely hitting the notes". Quantz was still the piper in a band, but he desperately wanted to join the royal musicians of Dresden. In the meantime, he learned what he could from these top-notch musicians.

When the Polish King's mother passed away, another 3-month ban on music was ordered. Quantz, as they say, made lemonade out of lemons by seizing the opportunity to travel, to soak in music from other cultures. He visited Silesia, Moravia, Austria and Prague during this time. While in Vienna, Zelenka again taught the young man counterpoint.

It's amazing how opportunities fell into Quantz' lap when other people might have seen a roadblock. No sooner had he switched to the "flute transversiere", than he realized, as mentioned before, that there was very little literature available for that instrument.

It is also amazing how greatness seems to meet greatness. His friend, Johann Georg Pisendel, the concertmaster, had met Vivaldi some years earlier on a trip to Italy. Vivaldi had dedicated many works to Pisendel. Quantz was certainly rubbing shoulders with an elite group of highly talented musicians.

Quantz' entry into composing shaped the sensitive style of music in Germany. The new style was less scholarly, less complicated and became much shorter and lighter in mood, and more accessible to amateurs.

Italian operas were introduced to Dresden in 1719. This gave Quantz the chance to study this art-form, the tonal ranges and the ornamental techniques.

In 1723, at the age of 26, the court allowed and paid for Quantz to travel to Prague for the coronation of Charles VI. This was also a learning opportunity since an opera, *Constanza e Fortezza*, was composed for that very event by Johann Joseph Fux. Quantz took notes and studied Fux' style.

7
Three Year Tour

It goes to show you, "it's who you know" and "who you get to know".

In 1724, Johann Joachim Quantz started his 3-year tour, sponsored and paid for again by the royal court of Dresden. The Count of Lagnasco traveled with Quantz. Quantz was 27 years old when he started this European tour.

First on the list was Italy. Quantz met Gaspirini, who taught him counterpoint. He was fortunate enough to meet a reluctant Alessandro Scarlatti who had just come back from Portugal. Scarlatti had no time for wind players, all of whom he considered to play out of tune. They discussed this fact which encouraged Quantz to think about ways to solve the intonation problem with the flute.

Then there was Johann Adolph Hasse who later became the Saxon Kapellmeister. Quantz took advice from them all and absorbed their teachings. He wrote down in his reports a great detail about techniques, voice pitches and skills in performance. Quantz met the renowned castrato, Farinelli, in Naples and to top it off, he met his musical idol, Vivaldi, in Venice.

It should be noted here that anybody who was anybody in those days spoke three or four languages. For the educated and the nobility, Europe was accessible by coach and boat and knowing several languages was essential. Frederick the Great, of course exceeded these basics. He not only spoke his native tongue, German, but also,

French, English, Spanish, Portuguese, and Italian. In terms of scholarly ability, Frederick also understood Latin, ancient and modern Greek, and Hebrew!

Johann Joachim Quantz was not expected to be a polyglot like Frederick who had privileged education. Yet, it would be easy for the musician to have picked up, at least, the practical languages in Europe, like German, French and English. After all, look at what he absorbed so easily in music! Quantz was one of those irksome people who could play any instrument on a whim and play it well.

In 1726, in Turin, Quantz was fortunate to meet the great violinist, Jean-Marie Leclair. Leclair became known as the Founder of the French School of Violin. They were the same age, 29, at the time and must have found this a charming coincidence. Maybe, Quantz saw Leclair's skill as a ballet dancer at the Turin theatre. There is not much recorded about their encounter. We do not know if Quantz met Giovanni Battista Somis who gave violin lessons to Leclair. Perhaps Quantz himself, took a few lessons from Somis on the violin. Somis had been a pupil of the great virtuoso and Italian composer, Arcangelo Corelli.

Quantz went on to France after his visit to Turin. He had royal permission and financial support to do this. The royal court must have been indulgent and also valued Quantz' ability greatly, hoping that its support would make the rising young star even more valuable among high musical circles.

Quantz heard Blavet and Naudot perform on the flute in Paris. They became friends of his and Quantz discussed ways to improve the flute. It was at this time in 1726 that Quantz added a second key (Eb, in addition to the standard D#) to help with intonation. This innovation was the beginning of modern flute making.

Lastly, in 1727, Quantz visited London, England on a three-month tour. He took in church music and opera performances. It must be noted that he met Frideric Handel there who tried to talk Quantz into staying in England. England had been good to Handel. However, it was time for Quantz to go back to Dresden, via Amsterdam, Hanover and Brunswick.

Quantz assessed his copious notetaking and what he had learned on his travels. He was inspired to develop his own compositional style. Not only did he write solo sonatas for the flute, but also trio sonatas for other instruments. His versatility was noticed.

8
Quantz is Noticed

Early in 1728, King Frederick William I traveled from Berlin to Dresden to the Polish court of Augustus II the Strong, Elector of Saxony and King of Poland.

Frederick William made the mistake of taking his 16-year-old son, Frederick [Junior if you will] with him. The Crown Prince was smitten with the fêtes, ballets and music there. He heard his first opera by Hasse's *Cleofide* and was impressed by the flute playing of Johann Joachim Quantz. It is ironic that the Crown Prince got to hear some of the finest court music through travels with his austere father who had no use for the arts or opera. [Ref: Exner dissertation, p.92]

The Crown Prince [later Fredrick the Great] wanted Quantz to leave his employment in Dresden and come to the Saxon court in Berlin. When Quantz visited Berlin, Queen Sophie Dorothea hired Quantz to teach the future King to play the flute.

However, the Crown Prince was only 16 years old at the time. Lessons were arranged in secret because the father squashed all "effeminate" pursuits. Frederick William 1 was a soldier's soldier, and he loved to drink. He had a bad temper. His idea of a man were ancient and rough.

Frederick William I was not happy to have his son play the flute, which seemed to be an unseemly activity for a man and a future King. The father figured that a King should have a warrior spirit like himself, and not be engaged in "soft" pursuits. It also seemed like all these soft pursuits were coming out of France at this time. He hated anything French!

In 1728, at the age of 31, Quantz put his violin and other instruments aside and concentrated solely on the flute. However, he walked into a hornet's nest when he took on the job of teaching the young Prince flute, having to do this in secret. Quantz accepted the job at great personal risk because King Frederick William I had not given his permission and had no time for musicians and useless artists who had their heads in the clouds.

The story goes that on one occasion Quantz and Frederick escaped detection by the skin of their teeth. Quantz and Frederick were warned in the last minute by Lieutenant Von Katte that the older King was on the warpath. Quantz, together with the flutes, music and music stands were bundled into a windowless cupboar while Frederick did a quick change from his French attire to his military dress uniform. He had no time to change his French-style hairdo though which the King hated.

While Quantz quaked inside the cupboard with Von Katte squeezed in there too, for a whole hour, the King found no sign of that flute player, Quantz, nor no sign of flutes. Quantz referred to this hiding place, in later years, as "the oven".

Quantz had been in "the oven", dressed in a red coat, a colour which the King also disliked. Red was a woman's color and also so French! In future years, when Quantz visited Berlin, he was careful to wear only grey or blue. During the rampage, the old King found his son's secret stash of books and French clothes. The clothes he threw in the fire; the books he demanded be auctioned off.

That year, in 1728, at the age of 16, Frederick decided to run away from home. He wanted to seek refuge with his uncle, King George I of England.

John Hartig Two Baroque Prodigies

Frederick set off in disguise, being helped by his faithful aide, Lieutenant Von Katte. They were intercepted. The father, King Frederick William I, was unforgiving. He saw the act as an act of treason. Frederick was tried for an offence which carried the death penalty. The King imprisoned the young man for a year and forced his son to witness the execution of his friend, the loyal Lieutenant Von Katte who was decapitated in front of young Frederick's eyes.

While in prison, the young Prince had his flute smuggled in so that he could practice. One wonders if the King ever found out about this deliberate continued disobedience.

At this time, the Crown Prince plummeted into a depression, refusing to eat. The father feared for his son's life and so gave in a little with a blind eye to the flute being smuggled into prison.

When young Frederick was released, the Crown Prince was granted his own residence from which he began to gather an entourage of great musicians, including Carl Philippe Emanuel Bach and Carl Heinrich Graun as Kapellmeister.

*****

One wonders what might have happened to a musician like Quantz in the wake of Kingly wrath.

Quantz was granted the privilege, however, to travel to Berlin twice a year by the Polish King to teach Frederick to play the flute and the basics of composition. That concession was probably granted because Prince Frederick refused to eat during his depression.

Overtures were made that Quantz should leave the services of Augustus the Strong of Poland and switch his musical services to the Saxon Court in Berlin and actually live there.

King Augustus refused to let Quantz go. The Crown Prince of Prussia would have to be satisfied with Quantz' twice yearly visit.

9
Frederick Grows Up

Thank goodness that the distance between Dresden and Berlin was only 100 miles. That trip was manageable in the middle of winter in January 1728. When they got there, the Polish King, Augustus II, had a continuous round of amusements planned out for his royal visitors from Berlin. The stay to young Frederick's father would be an insufferable four weeklong endurance of music, festivities ballets and opera. The Prussian King felt trapped. This was not the case with the Crown Prince, however, young Fritz! He experienced several of his firsts!

Augustus II was amused. He was a Catholic who could have fit well into the profligate times of the Roman Empire. He resolved to test his Prussian visitors with strategically arranged temptations. Frederick William spurned them. However, young Fritz fell, like a young man so willingly will.

Most likely it was Augustus who arranged for one of his beautiful mistresses to seduce the 16-year-old Frederick. This would be another first for the young Crown Prince, his first sexual encounter. How could a young man full of life and vigor resist the temptations "in the person of one of Augustus' beautiful mistresses." *[Exner dissertation, p.91]*

His father was probably talking boring politics with one of the Polish King's ministers while other things were going on secretly behind his back.

Young Fritz was very handsome, full of life. The mistress who was sent to seduce him thought it would be a pleasing pastime. Augustus' would think it was a great joke to play on the stuffy King Frederick Sr.

Who knows what the name of Augustus' beautiful mistress was? She did her assignment too well which probably came back to the Polish King as a laughable little story about how the Crown Prince of Prussia performed in the bedroom. The story is now forgotten, lost in the secret of an old bedroom.

A private room had been reserved. The mistress took young Frederick by the hand, an audacious move to touch royalty. She was so pretty that Frederick did not mind.

She engaged him in small talk.

"What interests your Highness?"

"Music mostly," he said.

"Would you like a royal court someday like the Polish King's where you can have operas and chamber music?"

"Yes, especially chamber music. I like the sound of the flute."

"Then, perhaps your father could arrange for our court flautist, Herr Quantz, to visit you for lessons. The Polish royal Highness speaks highly of his playing."

"Yes, I heard him in Hasse's opera, my first."

She gently pulled young Frederick towards the bed. He acquiesced.

"Have you ever...?" she asked.

Frederick swallowed hard. He was not especially aroused. He was more curious as to where this would lead. Maybe, it was like an experiment. There were many firsts in the young Prince's life, the courtly festivals, the opera, the chamber music. He felt fortunate to have experienced such delicious sights and sounds.

She pulled him even closer. His hand brushed her breast and went inside with her guidance. She felt his reluctance.

Suddenly, it all became clear to her.

"I see," she said, "you feel uncomfortable with women. You prefer young men?"

Frederick did not say anything; he did not want to reveal too much of his inner fears.

"It's all new to me."

"Don't worry, my little one," she said, "I will teach you how."

She took him in hand and helped him to mature in another matter in which he had little experience.

He came out of the chamber flushed and privately ashamed. His father must never know. He got the mistress to promise never to say anything to anybody.

However, she had already promised to come back to Augustus II with the story. The Polish King laughed during the anecdote but decided that it would remain hush, hush. One would not want a war with the Prussian King. Such matters were delicate.

Historian, John Abbott, writes that young Frederick's dissipation during the four weeks in Dresden, "left an indelible stain upon his reputation." [Abbott, p.52] But more than that, "Upon his return to Potsdam he was seized with a fit of sickness, and for many years his health remained feeble." [Abbott, p.52]

John Abbott goes on to say that Frederick's father found out about how his son was seduced and how he behaved in the Polish King's court. The father, who previously disapproved of his son, now loathed him, "in almost insane ebullitions of rage." [Abbott, p. 52]

There is no concern it seemed from the father as to why his son was so sickly after the Dresden visit. There is no scholarly guess that the problem might have been a sexually transmitted disease, perhaps even syphilis. We will never know.

10
Fritz meets Quantz

The opera, *Cleofide*, with its spectacle of music, singing and costumes, so impressed young Frederick, that the boy wanted to meet the composer, Johann Adolf Hasse. Actually, that was only a means to get to meet the flute player by whom he was so impressed, Johann Joachim Quantz.

When the Polish King heard of young Frederick's wishes, he was more than willing to comply and brought the composer, Hasse, to the royal court. Perhaps, there was some political advantage to acceding to young Frederick's wishes, a favour that Augustus could cash in on, on a later day.

"We have here a young admirer," said King Augustus to Hasse. Frederick explained how he had been impressed by the story behind the opera.

"Yes, I especially liked Alexander the Great showing mercy to the Indian King, Poros, after his invasion. I also liked how the wife of Poros made the plot complicated by making advances to Alexander."

"Human nature is confusing," admitted Hasse. "You do me honour by liking my opera."

"I would also like to meet the flute player, Herr Quantz, whose playing was so full of emotion."

"That can be arranged Your Majesty," said Hasse. "It will be done tomorrow. You are here for four weeks?"

"Good!" interjected the Polish King. "Tomorrow it is then. Quantz will be here at your service."

"Oh," said young Frederick, "and instruct Herr Quantz to bring his flute, also an extra if he has one."

The Polish King thought, "Quantz will be used in this chess game of power between Dresden and Berlin. I see possibilities."

*****

The next day involved not only a meeting with Johann Joachim Quantz but also a flute lesson.

Quantz was an impressive man; he was tall and stout, like a tradesman, a blacksmith, perhaps. Quantz pulled his flute out of his coat pocket. In fact, he had brought two.

"May I?" asked the young Fritz.

Quantz handed the boy the extra flute. He took it and held it to his mouth the way he had seen Quantz do in the opera. He blew. A squeal came out.

"Not as easy as one thinks," observed Quantz. "The mouth must be puckered, like so. It is called an embouchure."

Young Frederick tried again and got a tone out of the flute. His eyes sparkled with delight.

"I want to take flute lessons from you," said Frederick.

"I'm sure that can be arranged if His Majesty, Augustus, allows it."

Quantz bowed his head towards the Polish King who nodded back.

"Perhaps, we can arrange something on loan," the King suggested. "After all, 100 miles between Dresden and Berlin is not too far to go for flute lessons. Ask your mother or father about such a possibility."

Quantz was delighted with the boy's enthusiasm. He was a small lad, and someone who showed musical promise. After all, not everyone could evince a sound out of a flute on the first or second try.

Quantz looked forward to going to Berlin to give the boy lessons.

He and young Frederick had something in common. Before his teens, Quantz had been a small boy himself, so he saw himself in young Fritz. Now, that Quantz had outgrown his small stature and grew into the man that his father, the blacksmith, might be proud of, he felt protective of a boy like young Fritz, so small and thin in physique. He remembered his days of being bullied as a small and weak boy.

"I will be pleased to give Your Majesty flute lessons," he said again.

When young Fritz got home, he told his mother, Queen Dorothea, all about the Dresden experience, talking about the festivals, the ballets and the opera.

"And above all, mother," he said, "there was this flute player who played so sublimely that it entered my mind to take flute lessons from him."

"This may be difficult to arrange," said the mother, "you know how your father hates anything of the arts, if it has nothing to do with soldiering."

The mother said she would "arrange things". By this she meant that her husband, the Prussian King, would not be told about young Frederick's lessons. That it would have to be done in secret. Quantz would be sent for and instructed to bring an extra flute.

Young Fritz was delighted.

"The flute has such a lovely sound. It is like a mythical nymph singing."

"Let's not hear anything about a nymph," said the mother. "You are too young for that."

Queen Dorothea sent a letter to Augustus II to have Quantz come to Berlin twice a year to give her son lessons in the flute. Frederick and the flute were to realize a destiny together.

11
Dorothea Queen Mother

Frederick the Great's mother was Sophia Dorothea of Hanover. Sophie Dorothea loved her little Fritz tenderly, and, with a mother's fondness, endeavored to shield him, in every way in her power, from his father's gruff, soldierly manner. Sometimes, the Emperor could be brutal! *[John Abbott, Frederick the Great, 1871]*

Even though Frederick William I was faithful to her as a husband and indeed showed her affection, the man had a short temper when he was disobeyed, especially with his servants and his children. He would lash out and beat them.

Queen Dorothea feared his unpredictable temper. She also resented the fact that she had no influence at court and that her husband refused to get her children married off to their English cousins. The mother of young Fritz was the daughter of George I of England. Her brother subsequently became George II. Intermarriage in such alliances was crucial to the geopolitical balance of European powers.

Frederick the Great took after his mother in gifts and temperament. She promoted his artistic inclinations, especially when he wanted to learn how to play the flute. The father wanted his son to be a man's man. He forbad any of his son's artistic pursuits and his habit of wearing French fashions.

When young Frederick said he wanted to learn how to play the flute, it was Queen Dorothea who arranged to have Johann Quantz visit Berlin twice a year to give lessons. She did this secretly.

She had an independent spirit and often spurred her husband on in defiance to his wishes. Yet, they had 14 children together. Including the future King, Frederick the Great.

*****

"Our Frederick is different. He loves to read; he loves music, and he wants to play the flute. Why can't you let him be himself?"

"Being King does not allow you to be yourself. There are wars to be fought, money to be raised, treaties to be signed. Young Frederick must be tough as a Monarch."

"But he is still a boy at 16. Allow him some expression of his artistic nature."

"Artistic nature? If I see him with a flute, I'll break that thing in two! I will beat that artistic nature out of him."

Queen Dorothea turned around in a huff. She swept out of the room leaving her husband with his royal concerns over wars and treaties. She sent a courier to Dresden to ask the regent of Poland, Augustus II, if he could send Johann Quantz to Berlin to give young Frederick flute lessons. She would relay to Quantz when he arrived that the lessons would be given in the highest secrecy.

"Could Quantz bring an extra flute?" she instructed in the missive.

Thus, arrangements were made so that young Frederick could play music and be himself in secret.

12
Domineering Father

The old King was known as the "barracks King". He instructed his son's tutors to train him in the hard life. The Crown Prince must deny himself operas, comedies, and other follies of the laity. *[Andrea Kapell Loewy]*

The rigorous militaristic education started when poor Frederick was just a mere child. His father woke the small boy up to the sound of a cannon. When he was all of 6 years of age, the boy was given his own regiment of children to drill like a military sergeant. At the age of 7, he was given a miniature arsenal to whip into shape! *[wiki-Frederick William I of Prussia]*

All this was wasted on a little boy who was artistically inclined and who loved music and poetry.

> This rude, coarse discipline was thoroughly uncongenial to the Crown Prince. He was a boy of delicate feelings and sensitive temperament. The poetic nature very decidedly predominated in him. He was fond of music, played the flute, wrote verses, and was literary in his tastes. He simply hated chasing boars, riding on the sausage car, and being drenched with rain and spattered with mud. *[John Abbot, Frederick the Great, 1871]*

The old King was not averse to music as such, in the sense that a royal court should have a "kapelle" but only as an outward symbol of noble prestige. That served a practical purpose, but for a Crown Prince to actually write poetry or play music himself! That was, to Frederick William I, not a Kingly thing to do!

The domineering father disapproved of his son's studies in music, questionable books, fancy dressing gowns and fancy hairstyles! The son preferred French fashions to Germany's military style. The father, Frederick William, hated everything French! French was the language of philosophers, poets and avant-garde ideas, which he felt were useless luxuries to a militaristic monarch.

And yet, it was the father's hard work and domineering ways which made Prussia prosperous among the European powers. Young Frederick's father did some admirable things to improve the lot of all his subjects. It was the old man who made Prussia great again!

He was the one who recruited soldiers into the army who had to be taller than 6' into the regiment called the "langen Kerls", "long blokes". This is ironic in that the old King was a small man, as shown in the painting where Augustus II of Poland towered over him. *[portrait by Louis de Silvestre 1730]* It should also be noted that the son, Frederick the Great, was a small man at 5'3" tall.

The sheer number of men in the army also increased, giving many of the peasant class jobs. In 1713, Prussia's armed forces numbered 38,000. By the end of the old King's reign in 1740, he left his son an army of 83,000 men, with a war surplus of 8 million thalers! Prussia had become the third strongest military power in Europe, after Russia and France. In his younger naïve years, his son did not appreciate this. He did not realize his father's foresight and provisions in the kingdom!

*****

Although Frederick William I could be cruel in his private life, he showed a genuine concern for his subjects. He introduced several sweeping reforms. He got rid of his extravagant court. He also had Prussia's eastern territories resettled which had been ravaged and depopulated by the plague of 1709. This improved the lot of the peasantry. Frederick William freed the serfs completely by 1719. *[Britannica-Frederick William I of Prussia]*

He was convinced that an efficient state could not have illiterate subjects. He introduced compulsory primary education in 1717! The old King rearranged the way the tax system operated.

Overall, the old King left his son an efficient, centralized state with sound finances and a strong army. *[Britannica-Frederick William I of Prussia]*

Despite how awful the son made his father appear in his private home life where the young Crown Prince wanted to run away, his father indeed did many laudable things as an enlightened monarch in running a kingdom like a business.

13
Frederick's Sexuality

Scholars have surmised that Frederick the Great was homosexual. It's, of course, difficult to get any evidence in these private matters because, well, they are private. There is nothing surmised about Johann Joachim Quantz' sexuality because little in history has been said about that aspect of the man's private life. Frederick, on the other hand had more written about his proclivities because he was, after all the Emeror.

First of all, though this is not reliable, we must look at the stereotype. Here, I fly in the face of some poitical sensitivities.

Frederick was small; he was also highly gifted in the arts. There are of course homosexual body builders who look like wrestlers, but for this book, fine-featured and artistic traits put Frederick into a homosexual sub-category.

His father tried to correct these artistic tendencies by forbidding them and then storming through the castle to make sure his son was not wearing his French fashions and taking flute lessons from Quantz.

Both men, Quantz and Frederick, got married, but that does not mean anything in those days, especially among the nobility and highly gifted people. Alliances were arranged.

Quantz got married late, at the age of 40 which might indicate that he had no interest in women. He was tricked into marriage, and perhaps because he possibly could not perform in the bedroom, his wife, Anna Rosina, bullied him. There was no surprise that the marriage was childless.

Frederick also got married to Elisabeth Christine of Brunswick-Wolfenbüttel-Bevern. He was 21; she was 17. These are healthy ages for young people to produce offspring. The marriage too was childless!

Frederick's marriage was prearranged by the Austrian court as an alliance which would ensure peace between Austria and Prussia. The ceremony took place at the father in law's summer palace, his "Schloss Salzdhlum", in Wolfenbuttel.

It's sad that the relationship was cold and unfruitful. It is said that the Crown Prince spent "a reluctant hour" with his wife on their wedding night and then walked about outside for the rest of the night. *[wiki-Elisabeth Christine of Brunswick-Wolfenbuttel-Bevern]*

People would say that Frederick was lucky to get a young wife like Elisabeth Christine. That she was young and pretty. However, she was also religious and pious. And yet, because her husband had other proclivities, he shut her out.

Frederick had confided to his sister that, "There can be neither love nor friendship between us." *[wiki]* Certainly, Frederick gave her all the honours befitting her station, but never showed her any affection and apparently could not perform and produce an heir.

In 1740, after his father died, Frederick and Elisabeth Christine separated. She got the *Schonenhausen Palace* and the apartments at Berliner *Stadtschloss*. But she was forbidden from entering the royal court, *Sanssouci*, in Potsdam.

*****

And so, sadly, both Frederick and Quantz had unhappy marriages. Quantz was tricked, of course, but he had a choice not to fall for it. As it was, he had the option to divorce her, or if his religion did not permit, to live apart from Anna Rosina who hen-pecked the poor man.

On the other hand, Frederick, as a Crown Prince, had no choice. Everything was pre-ordained for him in the accepted alliances among royalty in those days. Frederick's status though and riches allowed him to buy off Elisabeth Christine with her own castle. Whereas he stayed at Sanssouci in Potsdam, ironically named "without worry" in French.

14
Liaisons

One wonders if there was ever anything sexual that happened between Quantz and Frederick. Nothing is to be found remotely hinting at that in the face of all those private flute lessons of them sitting side by side.

Perhaps, Quantz being 15 years older made him less attractive and Frederick being Quantz' pupil meant it was understood that they never would cross certain boundaries. Friendship and flute lessons were all that was to it between the two.

However, there is more basis for romantic speculations between Frederick and several other acquaintances throughout the Crown Prince's lifetime.

Frederick's sister, Wilhelmine, wrote about a suspected tryst between Frederick who was 16 at the time and a 17-year-old page named Karl Christoph von Keith. "I had noticed that he was on more familiar terms with this page, than was proper in his position, I did not know how intimate the friendship was." *[wiki...sexuality]*

Suspicions and rumors apparently slipped to the father's ears who did not like what he heard about his son. The father beat Frederick in public and humiliated him, trying to make a man out of him, wanting him to be more soldierly. Keith was fired and sent away to a regiment at the Dutch border, while Frederick was sent to Wusterhausen "to repent for his sin". *[wiki...sexuality]*

The most notable liaison came in 1729 or 1730 when Frederick, as an 18-year-old, got to know Hans Hermann von Katte who was 26 at the time. Von Katte was a lieutenant in the Prussian Army.

Von Katte was a boyish looking young man, with fine features and a thin build. He, unfortunately, had the misfortune of becoming Frederick's best friend.

Being 8 years older, von Katte had the advantage of more years of experience and also schooling. He had studied French and law at Koningsberg and Utrecht before joining the Prussian army. It is said that they both attended private mathematics and mechanics lessons together in 1729. Frederick was attracted to his friend's "cosmopolitan attitude". They both were interested in poetry and playing the flute.

It was about this time that the famous hide-out incident from a rampaging King took place where Quantz with his flutes and music stands, and von Katte, hid in a tiny hot cloakroom for an hour while old Frederick William I stormed through Frederick's chamber digging up books and clothes of Frederick's that he disapproved of.

Young Frederick had been humiliated enough by his father with the public scolding and beatings. He decided to run away from home, not an unheard-of thing for a disgruntled teenager to do. Except he was royalty, and the consequences had political ramifications.

Frederick had persuaded von Katte, his best friend, to help him run away to England to his uncle George, King of England, on his mother's side. A letter was intercepted. The two young men were arrested and thrown into prison in Kustrin.

The old King, soldier first and father second, saw the attempt to run away as desertion, an act of treason. He also suspected that the two might have plotted to seek military aid from the English uncle and come back to Germany to depose him.

Von Katte was found guilty of desertion. At first, his sentence was life imprisonment. But Frederick William overrode this and unilaterally changed the sentence to the death penalty. The old King argued that if von Katte were let off with a lighter sentence, then the King's Guard could never be trusted again. An example had to be made of von Katte! Young Frederick pleaded with his father, only to be ignored.

Frederick was forced from an upper window to watch the execution of his best friend, carried out with a long sword which beheaded the young lieutenant. Frederick stretched his hands out to von Katte below, pleading for forgiveness for getting von Katte into this mess, saying in French, "Please forgive me, my dear Katte, in the name of God, forgive me." Frederick fell to the floor in a faint as the sword came down on von Katte's neck.

Von Katte had written a farewell letter to his father. It expressed regret for his wasted upbringing and education, with "all the hopes for my future welfare". That there would be nothing to present his father with "the fruits of my efforts and my achieved sciences." "All in vain." That he has to "walk the path of disgrace and shameful death." Von Katte trusted that God was with him. He ended the letter by thanking his father, "with filial respect for all the father loyalty shown to me, from the childhood to the present hour." "Your faithful, until death, son. Hans Hermann." *[wiki-re. von Katte]*

*****

Frederick went into a deep despair for three days. He never spoke of von Katte again nor visited his grave.

Historians surmise that von Katte's romantic liaison with young Frederick probably had a role to play in the young lieutenant's death penalty. There was also the fact that he was 26 years old, and perhaps should have known better than to go along with an immature teenager in a plot to run away. After all, he was an officer, a lieutenant in the Prussian army.

15
Von Katte

"I am so angry at my father, I could spit," said young Frederick, the Crown Prince. "I am 18 and he still beats me in public and belittles me in front my classmates."

"I don't know what to say," commented von Katte. "Your father is the King and must be obeyed."

"Not when he is such a tyrant. He forbids me at every turn in things that make me happy. He wants me to be like him, a soldier, but I am not like him."

"You are trapped. You are the Crown Prince."

"I've been thinking of running away. I won't be the first to run away from an unhappy home."

"Where will you go?"

"I'm hoping that Uncle George in England will take me in. I can live in exile for a while until I become King. Then I can do what I want."

"That is if your uncle is willing to take you in."

It happened that Frederick's uncle advised his nephew not to run away, to stay in Germany and simply ride out the storm with the uncompromising father. Frederic did not realize in his youth how he would upset the delicate power balance in the European geopolitical scene if he succumbed to his adolescent wish to simply run away from home. There was more to the big picture in this scheme than for a teenager to simply run away from home.

The father, Frederick William I, was furious when a valet handed him a compromising letter which King George of England had addressed to his son.

"Do not come to England. Do not run away. Your father will be furious, not only with you, but also with me."

This tipped Frederick William I off to spy more closely on his son's plans. The father made rounds throughout the castile. Who was his son seeing, talking to, who were his friends? The father's suspicions were heightened when young Frederick kept company with Hans Hermann von Katte.

"Poetry, they like poetry? They are also reading French authors. I hear nothing good about that effeminate Voltaire! France is a degenerate country!"

The father became more entrenched in his views. "We are Christians. Next thing you know, homosexuality will be an accepted practice. I will put a stop to that. Frederick has to stay away from these 'schwul', effeminate tendencies. I will make a man out of him yet, even if I have to beat it into him."

A valet knew who, as they say, buttered his bread. He brought the letter from the King of England intended for Frederick to Frederick's father. The father's colour turned red when he glanced through the missive not intended for him.

"Frederick intends to run away from home. Seek refuge with my brother-in-law in England! Perhaps, they will hatch a plot to overthrow me."

Frederick William had his son arrested immediately. "That will cool his heels. Maybe a diet of bread and water will bring him into reality." Frederick William saw this running away business as desertion from the army, a treasonable offence, and he set the wheels in motion which would find his son, and his co-conspirator, Hans Hermann von Katte, guilty. They both were in the Prussian army and desertion was a serious matter.

Through the political grapevine, the old King found out that von Katte had certain "proclivities" which were "schwul" [gay] in the King's opinion. This had to end.

His son would face jail-time for a whole year to teach him a lesson. He could not be executed, however, because he was, after all, the Crown Prince.

But von Katte? That was another matter. As an officer, as lieutenant in the Prussian army, as someone not 18 but 26, he was clearly a deserter and a traitor. The old King decided to change von Katte's penalty from life imprisonment to the death penalty. An arrangement was made to have one of Prussia's best executioners with the broad sword engaged for the unpleasant task.

When Frederick heard of the final decision, he wrote von Katte a long letter. It basically asked for his forgiveness, that Frederick was unfair taking advantage of the lieutenant's friendship to fall in line with an immature plan, poorly thought out by himself, to help a Crown Prince run away from home.

Frederick felt contrite, not because he wanted to run away from home, but because he had brought his best friend into a stupid plan which would cost him his life. Frederick said repeatedly in his letter, forgive me, forgive me, forgive me.

On the final day of the execution, on a chilly November 6, 1730, the father made sure that his son got a front row seat from a top window overseeing the courtyard where he could watch his friend, von Katte, lose his head.

Von Katte was kneeling dressed in simple breeches and a shirt hanging loosely from bare shoulders. The neck was exposed for the sword which was held by the executioner behind him. The last rights had already been said by the priest standing there solemnly in black. The old King stood by, perhaps perversely enjoying his son pleading with outstretched arms at the window above to spare his friend's life. But justice was unforgiving. Von Katte lost his life that chilly November day for merely being willing to help a teenage friend escape the father's tyranny.

[wiki-von Katte old painting of decapitation]

16
Life Goes On

As an 18-year-old, the Crown Prince eventually pulled out of his doldrums. Apparently, he had his flute smuggled to him in prison which helped. As previously suggested, maybe, the father ignored knowing about this because he didn't want his son to starve himself to death because of a hunger strike.

As they say, life must go on. Eventually, young Frederick became intimate with another love interest when he and Michael Gabriel Fredersdorf corresponded romantically.

Fredersdorf became Frederick's valet. Later, when Frederick ascended the throne in 1740, he granted Fredersdorf an estate and asked him to act as unofficial prime minister. *[wiki re. sexuality]*

Historians also point to Frederick's possible liaison with none other than France's philosopher, Voltaire, in whom Frederick had an interest in later years. Frederick had asked Voltaire to come live with him at *Sanssouci*. However, Frederick found Voltaire difficult to live with in person because the egos clashed.

Voltaire was an inflammatory individual and attacked the President of Frederick's academy in the form of a pamphlet with an insulting title, *Le Diatribe du Docteur Akakia*. Frederick burned the pamphlet publicly and put Voltaire under house arrest. *[wiki re. sexuality]*

Voltaire left Prussia but took a bunch of poems with him written by Frederick in which Frederick mocked other rulers. Frederick sent his agents to detain Voltaire in

Frankfurt and forced him to give the poems back. This episode has been called a "lover's quarrel". Eventually, Voltaire and Frederick resumed their friendship and their correspondence continued over a span of 50 years.

In 1739, Frederick met the bisexual Venetian philosopher, Francesco Algarotti. They were attracted to each other. Algoretti held the opinion that northern Europeans lacked passion, so Frederick wrote an erotic poem, which suggested an orgasm, "La Jouissance".

> *This night, vigorous desire in full measure,*
> *Algarotti wallowed in a sea of pleasure.*
> [cit. Kathryn Hadley in History Today]

Frederick also filled his palaces with erotic artworks that reflected his longing for homosexual relationships. Many of these hailed back to Grecian Myths and Legends.

17
The Old King Dies

The hostility between father and son, between Frederick William I and Frederick the Great, stretched out for years. Young Frederick never quite forgave his father for making him watch the execution of Hans Hermann von Katte.

The father had his son marry Princess Elisabeth Christine of Brunswick-Bevern whom Frederick despised. As the years rolled by, young Frederick came to understand some of the difficult decisions that his father had to make, juggling the balance of power in Europe.

Once young Frederick agreed to marry Princess Elisabeth Christine, he, at least, was allowed to indulge in his music and literary interests. He was also given a stud farm to raise horses in East Prussia and given the Rheinsberg Palace as concessions.

Frederick later admitted that his father, "penetrated and understood great objectives and knew the best interests of his country better than any minister or general." *[wiki-Frederick William I of Prussia]* Despite the years of abuse that Frederick endured from his father, Frederick could see some of his father's wisdom in dealing with matters of state. Maybe, the father could have handled his son with a more moderate approach. But then, old Frederick was irascible and stuck in his ways.

The father had wanted his son to be more manly and to be disciplined like a soldier. When Frederick hid books on

French philosophers, the father erupted in bouts of anger when Frederick was a teenager. He would physically attack servants with a cane, even his own children, with Frederick often in his line of sight. The old King also suffered from gout which contributed to his outbursts. He hated France immensely because of its liberal philosophies. Therefore, when the Crown Prince got interested in French philosophy and literature, the old King got very angry. Things remained strained and unsaid between father and son, right to the very end.

Frederick William I died in 1740.

We do not know if Frederick ever reconciled with his father, probably not. The execution of the Crown Prince's best friend in 1730 was unforgiveable in Frederick's mind.

18
No Reconciliation

Frederick William I was only 51 when he died in 1740. On his deathbed, the father asked for his son to forgive him.

"I only did it for your good," he said. "I had to teach you hard lessons so that you would be a real King to your subjects."

"Those lessons could have been taught without the caning and your yelling," said Frederick.

"Can you imagine what would have happened to the kingdom, if I would have let myself go, to indulge in music and going to plays? The warring countries of Europe would have laughed at us."

"I admit that you have strengthened Prussia. The peasants are happier now. There are jobs in the army; it is strong. We have a good economy. But father, we could have had a happier home life."

"Why won't you forgive me?" asked the old King.

"You know why," said Frederick.

"Was it von Katte?" asked the King.

"Yes. The young man could have been granted clemency. He was only following my requests to get away from you."

"I saw that as desertion, and besides, von Katte was 26 years old. He should have known better than to be persuaded by a mere boy to flee to England to seek refuge there."

"Perhaps, it could have been handled differently. Won't you forgive me for my strictness?"

"No!" said Frederick firmly. "I saw you as a tyrant and cruel. There was no mercy in what you did to poor gullible von Katte."

"It had to be done. Von Katte was an officer in the Prussian army. He knew the consequences."

The King moved painfully in his bed. His breath came in rasps. His energy was waning away as he talked with his son.

"But more than anything else," said the old King, "was that sinful liaison you had with von Katte. There were rumors of a romantic tryst between the two of you. That was an abomination in the Bible. It might have repeated itself had I granted von Katte clemency. Imprisoning the young man for life would also not have solved the problem. You would still have sought him out in jail."

"But father, we did not see it that way. Can a leopard change its spots? We are born with our natures."

"I had hoped to beat that out of you."

"That's just the problem. You believed too much in that motto, spare the rod and spoil the child."

The father turned again in bed. His breath was belabored.

Young Frederick brought up the old King's restrictions on music.

"Why were you so furious about the flute and my lessons with Quantz? What is the harm in appreciating music? Even soldiers on the front like to hear old melodies which remind them of home."

"I had no objection to music as such. It only seemed openly effeminate for a King to play the flute, not a thing for a leader to do."

John Hartig   Two Baroque Prodigies

"Did you know that Quantz's father was a blacksmith? Quantz, himself, is tall and stout."

"I would rather have seen you on a horse whipping your soldiers in line, than being a pied piper to them."

"I wanted more to be a philosopher-king like Plato says, than a tyrant like Machiavelli says," countered Frederick.

"That all is water under the bridge," gasped the father. "Yet, forgive me my son."

"I cannot," replied Frederick, "perhaps, God will have it in his heart."

With that, the old King expired. Frederick walked away from the bed, his own heart hardened, shedding no tear, simply saddened that God had not granted him a softer father.

Frederick was also saddened that he had no wife in whom he could confide. Elisabeth Christine was sequestered in her castle at her own summer residence in the *Schonhausen Palace* in Berlin.

It was May 31, 1740. Farmers said it would be a hot summer. Frederick looked forward to the throne and to changing a few things in what was his kingdom now.

Meanwhile, his wife, Elisabeth Christine, heard about the old King's death, too late to attend his dying moments. The Crown Prince rarely communicated with her because he swore never to love her, the father having arranged the loveless marriage for political expediency only.

19
Quantz Gets Married

Johann Joachim Quantz was 40 years old in 1737 when he got married. He would have been happier had he remained a bachelor! As an ironic parallel, that was also the case with Frederick the Great, and indeed Jean-Marie Leclair.

Johann Joachim Quantz was already married to his job as a gifted musician. There is not much detail on his married life though, except that his wife, the widow Anna Rosina Carolina Schindler, tyrannized the big brute of a man. Half of Berlin gossiped about the unhappy marriage that Quantz got himself roped into. One can only speculate.

Why did he ever marry this "termagant"? She was not especially pretty, nor kind. The marriage was childless.

It seems that Quantz was tricked into the marriage. It all started when Quantz' horn-player friend, Schindler, died. Quantz visited the grieving widow to comfort her. She apparently took a shine to him and knew how to manipulate his visits.

On one occasion, she seemed terribly ill. Quantz called the doctor. The priest was called for the last rights. When asked what her dying wish was, she said she wanted nothing more than to go to her grave bearing the name of Mrs. Quantz.

Quantz thought he had nothing to lose, so he conceded, where upon she miraculously recovered having secured the comfort of a secure living. *[Rachel Brown article, 2010]*

John Hartig   Two Baroque Prodigies

Carl Philippe Emanuel Bach alluded one day to Quantz being afraid of his wife in a riddle posed to His Majesty, Frederick the Great at a party. Often, there is a grain of truth behind a so-called joke!

Bach described Quantz as "being the slave of his wife". Bach goes on to say Quantz was afraid of Madame Quantz, and Frederick, the greatest monarch in the world, was afraid of Quantz. *[Feike Bonnema quotes]*

It is noted that the king laughed heartily at this joke, all meant in good fun. Maybe Quantz chuckled a bit too at his public humiliation. But if Frau Quantz [Mrs.] was true to her nature, she probably gave Quantz an earful when they got home, even though he did not do anything wrong!

We do not know why Anna Rosina hen-pecked her husband. Maybe she was disgusted with his looks when he got undressed? Maybe he couldn't perform in the bedroom, her not being that attractive a woman with a sharp tongue.

If so, why did she ever focus on him? How did Quantz, such a gifted musician, descend into becoming a bullied husband? She tricked him into the marriage because she needed social security in the status-minded society of the times. Widows and orphans had it tough.

Maybe there was also his incessant time spent practicing that infernal flute! Tootling around the house might have irritated her. Maybe, she got sick of having to call him for supper!

No details come from the autobiography that Quantz himself published in 1755. There was nothing in it about private matters! The autobiography talked about his meteoric rise in music. His successes, his compositions and most particularly, his pecuniary rewards, how much he was paid by the nobility. He was proud of being the highest paid musician in the royal court. There was nothing about private matters and how he felt when his wife brow-beat him.

It is a human trait, even for women, to pick on someone who is weaker. Quantz' great-nephew, Albert Quantz, wrote about his great-uncle in detail in 1877, but again, there is a lack of personal revelations about the marriage.

Despite the wife's cruelty, we need to mention that she herself was a highly intelligent woman, one with a gift for painting, as seen in her self-portrait. From the looks of her self-portrait, she must have been a no-nonsense person without a sense of humour, but one marked with a mean streak against her gentler, musical husband. She knew how to press his buttons.

*****

It's ironic that Frederick's own marriage was unhappy too, one of convenience, an accepted formality among nobility in those days. He lived apart from his wife and surrounded himself with intellectuals which included the likes of Voltaire.

Frederick and Elisabeth Christine had no children. Frederick bestowed the title of heir to the throne, Prince of Prussia, on his nephew when he died in 1786. The nephew was crowned Frederick William II. It seems like what goes around, comes around.

*****

One might say that Frederick the Great was married to his music, like Quantz was, although with time, Frederick became adept as a military leader. On the music front, he earned a praiseworthy reputation in his chamber music as a soloist who could carry the melody with emotion and dexterity. Quantz seemed always to be at his side. Of course, if you are the monarch, then you can afford to have someone like Quantz at your side as your own personal tutor.

When the King's special chamber group met to play privately in the evenings, only highly skilled musicians, like C.P.E. Bach would have the audacity to make a sarcastic remark about His Majesty's playing, like when he was out of rhythm. Other than that, it was only Quantz who was granted the liberty to criticize the King's playing. This was usually done by a slight cough of correction or a Bravo if the passage was played really well by the King.

Both Quantz and Frederick settled into their "unhappy wedded bliss" after Frederick ascended the throne in 1740. Their music was their sanctuary. It gave them time away from their wives when they rehearsed together.

20
Bickering

The couple opened the door to their home silently. In fact, Anna Rosina had been giving Quantz the silent treatment all the way home in the coach. Neither one of them were happy with how things had gone at the party among his musical friends.

"You could have stopped Bach from telling his stupid riddle!" she accused.

"How? And humiliate him instead, the illustrious harpsichordist for His Majesty, the King?"

"Yes," she countered. "All you needed to say was, 'Enough is Enough'."

"To make me the butt of a joke!" she screamed at Quantz, finger pointing and shaking. "The very idea of me being afraid of my lapdog!"

"It was a stupid riddle anyway," countered Quantz. "No harm done. Even His Majesty laughed at it."

"No harm done! Me, and a lapdog, and you pictured as the fearful husband? What a public humiliation!"

"I admit that Bach's riddle was in bad taste, but what would you have me do? Slap the man in public and challenge him to a duel?"

"You could have stood up for me in other ways...even said, 'Stop! That will be enough!'"

The couple had been sleeping in separate quarters for some time now. Quantz regretted marrying her. She retired to her room where she kept her easel and her paints. She calmed herself by finishing a self-portrait. She was a good painter, perhaps not as good as Quantz was as a flute player, but nevertheless, she was good.

Quantz had a cubicle arranged in the house where he could retreat to think, to write and to play the flute when he wanted. The walls had been made sound-proof. Quantz' lucrative salary paid for the renovations.

The Bible says something about not letting the sun go down on one's anger. The couple never said good night to each other. Their separate doors remained closed.

In the morning, Quantz put his flute in its case and quietly exited the house. He hailed a coach to take him to his favourite coffee house. Wealthy citizens had been drinking coffee in Berlin since 1721.

It was Frederick William I, Frederick the Great's father, who had granted a foreigner the privilege of running a coffee house in Berlin, free of all rental charges. It was called "the English coffee house". It served the same purpose as the coffee houses in Paris, the most famous one being "Le Procope" where the intelligentsia sat and discussed grand ideas which could change the world and make your head spin.

In this case, in Berlin, Quantz just wanted to order his coffee to stimulate his mind and maybe a cake to settle his stomach. And to think about the argument from last night. He wished he could divorce his wife, but his Christian upbringing forbad that. "I guess I have to accept my punishment for being so stupid," he thought.

"She was right," he concluded. "I could have told Bach to shut up. His riddle was in poor taste."

He was hurt that Frederick, the Monarch, had laughed at the joke despite its hidden, hurtful barbs at Quantz, his wife and even the King! Bach had run close to the line of insulting the King, but then this was Frederick II and not

Frederick William I. If it were the father, there might have been hard consequences, even against Bach, the illustrious harpsichordist. After all, Von Katte had been beheaded by His Majesty's father for helping young Frederick to run away to England. That was considered treason, and with the old King, the plot reaped dire consequences. The death penalty! Maybe Bach should have reaped a good slap in the face for that riddle in poor taste!

Quantz satisfied himself with that revengeful thought, left the café and hailed a coach for the palace. He and the King had a flute lesson that morning, without Bach present.

21
Psychoanalysis

In the biography of Quantz by Feike Bonnema, Johann Joachim Quantz is described as "haughty" by none other than the Crown Prince himself. In a letter to his sister, Wilhelmina, dated January 12th, 1736. Frederick warns his sister that Quantz likes to think of himself as "a grand seigneur". She must not cater to how Quantz presents himself or to fall for his "airs".

> You will find Quantz high opinion of himself the more insupportable in that it is really without foundation. The only way to bring his haughtiness to an end is not to treat him too much like the grand gentleman. *[Feike Bonnema website]*

Even though, the Crown Prince might have exhibited the same picadillo of haughtiness because, after all, he was a Prince, nevertheless, he could spot it in others, and in a sense, be indulgent of that fault to a degree and know how to handle it, especially where Johann Joachim Quantz was concerned.

It all goes back to Quantz' childhood. With his perfect pitch and eidetic memory, he mastered a bunch of instruments easily and became quite confident in outperforming others. When other boys picked on him for his small size, in his early years, and his proclivity to do not considered "male", Quantz used his confidence as a shield of superiority against them. And indeed, he was superior to them!

Yet, deep down, there was a part of his psyche which suffered from an inferiority complex. That inferiority complex lurked deep inside his psyche even into adulthood.

He brandished his haughtiness as a shield against the world and those cruel people who sought to diminish him. It was his music which gave him solace, an area which no one could challenge because he did it so well. Yet, once in a while, that little boy who lurked in his past emerged and came to the surface with all the conflicting complexes of a little boy.

Perhaps Frederick the Great, his good friend, sensed all this and made allowances. He understood Quantz and accepted the man's faults. Quantz was too valuable to diminish and disrespect. He was favoured by the Gods, in a sense, like a Mozart. Among humanity, he must be respected, though some people were too blind or too ignorant to see the shining light of genius there. Lesser people must be ignored in Quantz' mind if they project cruel streaks which are not warranted in special abilities in themselves.

*****

Poor Quantz! He should never have married!

He was "roped in", according to modern cynics of the institution. Yes, he felt sorry for the widow Anna Rosina Carolina Schindler when her husband died. She feigned illness and said nothing would make her happier than to go to her grave as Madame Quantz. Quantz thought he was doing a good deed. He had nothing to lose; she was dying anyway. He gave up his happy bachelorhood of 43 years. If only someone would have warned him about the machinations of the opposite sex, or if something had happened to expose the conniving mind of the widow.

She recovered and brought out that fearful little boy in him. She knew how to press his buttons, as the saying goes. Johann Joachim Quantz faced a bully in his own household. He was trapped; he had taken the sacred oath 'til death do us part. One can only guess how he survived with her under the same roof. Nothing was ever written about his private life. Yet, he had his flute and his music as his refuge and his strength and a "man's cave" where he practiced.

In 1739, Quantz sunk himself into flute making, "to drill some of his own because of the lack of good flutes." Maybe, the work also took his mind off his criticizing wife. His pupil, Frederick the Great, owned 11 flutes made by Quantz.

It is known that, when Quantz sunk himself into his flute making or his practicing, he sequestered himself from his wife's quarters by making a separate soundproof cubicle for himself in his own house. There, in his own private little bubble, he could make his flutes in peace and also practice when the mood struck him.

*****

It should be noted that Quantz never joined the larger King's orchestra.

Quantz recalls in his autobiography, that he had, "the privilege of not having to play in the orchestra, but only in the smaller Royal chamber music, and not having to take orders from anyone but the King." *[Low, p.44]*

He was happy when his time could be spent in private chamber music sessions with Frederick in 1740 when His

Majesty actually became King of Prussia. The King took daily lessons from Quantz and preferred to engage in playing behind closed doors with his select group of chamber music specialists.

Quantz lived in Berlin-Mitte, the middle of Berlin on Kronenstrasse for the rest of his life. Quantz played at Frederick's royal court until his death in 1773 at the age of 76.

Charles Burney, the English music historian, visited the royal court in Berlin towards the end of Quantz' life. He considered Quantz to be, "an opinionated old pedant", full of his own ego. Burney felt that Quantz rested on his laurels at this stage of life, noting that Quantz's music was still being played from 40 years previously, but that the flautist had not kept up with the times.

22
Berlin

As previously said, Quantz' pupil and friend, Frederick, ascended to the Prussian throne to become Frederick II, aka Frederick the Great in 1740. Frederick was 28 years old.

The new King of Prussia did not let the Polish King deter him from winning Quantz over to the Saxon Court. King Frederick offered Quantz a salary he could not refuse, 2,000 thalers per year for life, with special payments for new compositions, plus 100 ducats for each flute that the man made. Quantz became the King's highest paid instrumentalist! Johann Joachim Quantz was 43 years old. Musically and socially, he had arrived!

Quantz moved from Dresden to Berlin. Soon, Berlin became the epicenter of music in Germany. While still a Crown Prince, Frederick had been networking with the top virtuosi, many of whom he eventually lured to Berlin when Frederick William First died in 1740. Quantz joined the King's royal court along with renowned names like C.P.E. Bach, Benda, Czarth, Graun, Hesse and Richter. There was a total of 17 musicians primarily devoted to chamber music who greeted Frederick when he finally ascended the throne. Frederick had been told by D'Alembert, "The philosophers and the men of letters in every land have long looked upon you, Sire, as their leader and model."

That idealistic talk was actually backed by force and military might! Frederick II could not have pursued his artistic goals were it not for the strong army and ample funds that his practical-minded father had left him. Frederick the Great would not have become Frederick the Great were it not for the provisions and the money his father had amassed.

As the new King, Frederick the Great took his place confidently in the geopolitical intrigue of 18th century Europe. It must be remembered that the father had done so much to solidify his son's status in Europe, while the son, in his early years did not appreciate that fully and instead, had the luxury of pursuing music and the arts secretly while his father attended to matters of state to strengthen the kingdom of Prussia.

*****

Frederick's plans went into action once he became the new King. He diverted huge sums of money to the Arts. A new opera house was built in Berlin; a separate building not confined to the royal court. It opened in 1742. Two opera series were produced each Carnival season.

One of the musical luminaries which the King brought to the royal court was, of course, Johann Joachim Quantz, along with other great musicians of the time. The King held concerts at his residence, *Sanssouci,* near Potsdam. He had become what Plato might call "a philosopher king."

Quantz was bribed, you might say, to leave the court of the Polish King in Dresden and come to Berlin with an outrageous salary. It was even higher than the famous son of Johann Sebastian Bach, C.P.E. Bach, got.

In the private little chamber music sessions, the composer and soloist always were Quantz or the King. Frederick was immersed in music, in a hands-on style. In fact, he wrote the libretti for the operas *Silla* in 1753 and *Motezuma* in 1755. *[Loewy article, 1990]*

Quantz enjoyed the private understanding he had with the King. Quantz had to report only to the King. He was also the only person allowed to make comments and criticisms about His Majesty's flute playing.

Quantz gave the King lessons almost daily. It was clear how important the flute had become to Frederick the Great. Kayla Low writes in her master's dissertation, that Lord Rosebery observed, "The flute was to Frederick what smoking is to the men of to-day. It filled up gaps in his time, soothed him, assisted meditation, and digestion." *[Low, p.44]*

Frederick was pleased to have Quantz conduct house concerts and compose music regularly for the flute. Quantz, in his private time, even published a book in 1752 of instructions on how to play the "flute transversiere". The book was called the *Versuch* [abbreviated because the title is so long in German]. Quantz dedicated the book to King Frederick the Great. The book was quite popular and was published in several European languages. It helps to have the right contacts! Jean-Marie Leclair likewise knew how to "network" because his publisher in Paris was a woman and they became lovers.

23
As Time Goes By

Musicians were a tradeable commodity in the 18th century among the nobility. You will lend me Bach and I will send you Quantz for a month. Apparently, Prince Frederick had an arrangement with his sister, Wilhelmine, when she wanted to take flute lessons from Quantz. She appreciated the man's talent. She wrote in a letter to her brother, Frederick, from Bayreuth in 1732: "It is so generous of you to provide me with concerts by Quantz. He is the god of music." *[Feike Bonnema quotes]*

When apparently the Prince and Quantz had a falling out in March 1734, she wrote: "It is very sad that you lost Quantz…you will never find his equal." Two years later, in 1736, she wrote: "Quantz is obedient as a lamb."

She also remarked that maybe the falling out had to do with Quantz being jealous of the King's playing in Ruppin. As suggested in a previous chapter, Quantz got annoyed that the Crown Prince allegedly played as well as he did. "He has told me that several times."

However, to say that the pupil played as well as the master could have been simple flattery, which was an expected practice used by those in service to the nobility. It is ironic that the Princess suggested jealousy as the cause to the friction between Frederick and Quantz. Typically, the jealousy is directed towards Quantz, not that Quantz is jealous, as suggested, of anybody else.

Nevertheless, the Crown Prince did play his flute very well. He played better than a dilettante and possessed a fine tone. The famous singer, Elisabeth Schmeling, said,

John Hartig   Two Baroque Prodigies

"He did not blow...like a King, but very well; he had a strong full sound and much virtuosity." *[Andrea Kapell Loewy]*

An objective observer, Charles Burney, praised Frederick for his sensitive playing.

Monarchs are the focus of flattery. It should be noted that C.P.E. Bach never lowered himself to this ploy. In fact, Bach could be downright rude or caustic in his remarks to the King. *[Andrea Kapell Loewy article]*

We have only to recall Bach's forwardness in making up that rude riddle he posed at a dinner party of select musicians where he suggested that His Majesty was afraid of Quantz, like Quantz was afraid of Mrs. Quantz. On another occasion, the King had his flute in hand, ready for a performance and asked innocently enough of the harpsichordist, C.E.P. Bach, "what rhythm?" Bach sarcastically replied, "what rhythms!" suggesting that Frederick could not keep time!

This reminds me of the friendly interchange between Kreisler and Einstein in their music making. Apparently when Einstein missed yet another entrance while playing in a quartet with Fritz Kreisler, Kreisler turned to him and asked, "What's the matter, professor? Can't you count?"

There is an understood leeway in minds trying to create music at that level. Some forgiveness is earned among gifted friends. Among the members of Frederick the Great's chamber music group, the King had his favourites. Bach was not one of them! But Bach had leeway to say certain things and get away with it. The King did get even with Bach in other ways. No sarcastic rejoinders as such but as Loewy pointed out in her article, "Bach's works were not included in the regular programs at either Sans-Souci or Berlin."

It is no doubt that Bach felt underappreciated. His salary was only 1/7th of what Quantz got. Quantz enjoyed 2000 thalers per annum, whereas Bach got 300. When rumblings through the grapevine in 1756 suggested Bach might leave Berlin, his salary was increased to 500 thalers but that was still far from Quantz' comfortable pay-scale. Musicians can be such a petty, competitive lot that it has always been difficult to keep them happy.

Quantz was discreet in how he showed his displeasure when His Majesty made a mistake on a piece. He'd cough quietly. When His Majesty made a mistake by playing a tritone accidentally during a performance, Quantz coughed quietly, "signaling C.P.E Bach to repeat the interval in the clavier to hide the mistake." *[Low, p.46]* At another time, it was amusing when His Majesty said to C.P.E. Bach, "We must not aggravate Quantz's cough." *[Andrea Kapell Loewy article]*

However, the Seven Years' War between 1756 – 1763 put an end to Frederick's flute playing. He had no time for the flute when he waged war with Austria and Great Britain. Frederick had to attend to matters of state to which his more practical minded father was better suited.

Yet, Frederick seemed to have adapted and had become a strategist in politics after his father died in 1740 at a reasonably young age of 51. Frederick II sent troops into Silesia to prevent Austria from retaking the territory.

It was Frederick who set the stage for German unification. In his later years, he earned the title of "der alte Fritz", "old Fritz". *[wiki-Frederick the Great]*

During the Seven Years' War, Frederick the Great had a strong enough army to capture Dresden, Quantz's old residence under the Polish King. Now Quantz lived in Berlin under the protection of Frederick the Great and thrived there with a salary which exceeded even that of C.P.E. Bach.

The years had ravaged Frederick's health and his flute lay neglected. He lacked control of his breath, had a few missing teeth and his gout hurt his concentration.

In 1779, the monarch told Franz Benda, one of his violinists, "My dear Benda, I have lost my best friend." *[Andrea Kapell Loewy article]*

Actually, when the King had commented to Benda in 1779, that he had lost his best friend, meaning his flute, it could also refer to Quantz who died six years earlier in 1773.

One wonders how well His Majesty could really play. Some scholars have suggested that Quantz' compositions met the needs of someone below the virtuoso level, i.e., for a sub-par flutist. As Kayla Low suggested, "As Frederick was the ruler of one of the greatest empires at the time, it is difficult to separate loyalty to the crown from his actual flute playing dexterity." *[Low, p.47]* Low comments that Frederick's skill level caused Quantz to become known for his simple, unoriginal compositional output which was specifically geared for the King's level of playing to make him seem better than he was. *[Low, p.47]*

The Seven Years' War, fought in Europe and North America, killed the music scene in Berlin. Key musicians left Frederick's entourage, first Christoph Nichelmann, the second harpsichordist in 1756, then C.P.E. Bach in 1767. No operas were staged. After the war ended, all productions were of previously written works. Frederick stopped composing. He no longer played the flute.

Quantz died earlier than His Majesty in 1773, at the age of 76. There are few details about how he died or about his funeral. When Quantz died, all his manuscripts became property of the King. That is why they survived, and we have copies of them today.

The monarch himself died at *Sans Souci*, the castle "without worry" in 1786, at the age of 74.

24
The Wives

Johann Joachim Quantz's Wife:

Anna Rosina Carolina Schindler tricked Quantz into marrying her, saying that she would like nothing better than to be Mrs. Quantz before dying. She was supposedly on her deathbed, so Quantz figured he'd make the poor woman happy. He said sadly, "Yes". She recovered and made his personal life hell because she hen-pecked him.

Poor Quantz should have remained a bachelor. We do not know for sure if they had separate apartments in their house in Mitte-Berlin, on Kronenstrasse. We can assume so. After all, Quantz's best friend, Frederick had separated from his wife by giving her her very own palace, and so they lived apart for most of their married life. Quantz, of course, could not afford such a luxury. It's a wonder that there was no divorce. Perhaps, Quantz' religious belief forbad divorce and the marriage simply drifted on as a "status quo".

All of Berlin apparently knew that Quantz was tyrannized by his wife. There was room for gossip. C.P.E. Bach came up with that riddle at a party where Quantz and even His Majesty were made the butt of a joke about who was afraid of whom in this insulting jibe.

Googling high and low, I could not find when Mrs. Quantz died or what happened to her.

Meanwhile, Frederick the Great's Wife:
*It should be noted that Elisabeth Christine, Frederick's wife, the Crown Princess of Prussia, is not to be confused with another Elisabeth Christine Ulrike, the mother of Queen Maria Teresa.

*****

Frederick the Great's wife, Elisabeth Christine, was quite intelligent. She authored translations of works in political literature under a pseudonym, "Constance". She also did a lot of charity work during the Seven Years' War 1756 to 1763. She contributed more than half of her income, 23,000 thalers out of her 40,000 thaler allowance to the poor and injured. Quite an admirable woman!

In 1763, when Frederick saw her for the first time in six years, he insultingly remarked, "Madame has grown quite fat." *[wiki-Elisabeth Christine of Brunswick]* That was a cruel and unthinking remark for Frederick to make. Sad, they had nothing kind to talk about.

She was the one who carried out ceremonies and greetings for the nobility at court. At her summer residence, Schonhausen Palace, in Berlin, Elisabeth received foreign princes, ambassadors and generals. She entertained with concerts and held receptions.

However, Frederick inherited one quality from his father which was to be Spartan with the royal funds, so that Princess Elisabeth did not always have the money to pay for gala events. The King rarely attended any court events, so that she was left alone to represent the Prussian monarchy. She did a good job in this with limited funds.

Understandably, when Frederick II died in August 1786, she was not present at his death. She commented about her husband to his successor, nephew Frederick William II: "He was generous and beneficent, he maintained his position without hauteur, and in society he was like a private gentleman."

[wiki/Elisabeth_Christine_of_Brunswick-Wolfenbüttel-Bevern]

She was called "queen dowager" after Frederick's death. In his will, Frederick provided for her income, even for her wines and the firewood for her royal palaces. There was a directive that the successor, the nephew Frederick William II, treat her with respect. She was often consulted in the affairs of court.

When Frederick died in 1786, he was 74 years old. The queen dowager, his wife, died in 1797 at the age of 81.

25
Death of Quantz

Johann Joachim Quantz died in 1773 at the age of 76. It was a good age for someone who was living in the 18th century in Europe.

The King arranged a respectful burial for his private musical tutor. They had known each other for 45 years since Frederick was 16 and Quantz was 31. It was a long and fruitful relationship.

We know when Quantz died, which was on July 12, 1773, but we do not know any details about his ailment or if he spoke a farewell on his deathbed to Frederick the Great. One of the internet biographies says, "It is a credit to Quantz in creating compositions which featured the flute at an earlier time when the instrument would have been overwhelmed by other woodwind instruments." [new world encyclopedia-Johann Jakob Froberger article]

*****

"How is he doing Herr Doktor?"

"Not well, your Majesty, not well."

Frederick opened the door to Quantz' apartment on Kronenstrasse. Mrs. Quantz stood silently in one corner of the bedroom. She curtsied when His Majesty entered the darkened room.

Frederick took Quantz' wrinkled hand. "Well old friend," he said, "we've seen better days."

"Yes, Your Majesty."

Quantz chuckled, then coughed. It was a hot July evening. He could hear the birds twittering an evening song outside his window. Perhaps, he thought, it was a funeral choir for him.

"It's been a pleasure," he said, "teaching you how to play the flute."

"I could not have done with a better teacher than you, my old friend."

Quantz told His Majesty that there were half a dozen new flutes he had in the closet in his study. His Majesty was welcome to have them, "as a memento".

Frederick merely nodded his head to a valet who rushed off to the study to seek out the flutes.

"I shall treasure them," commented the King who himself was feeling his age. Frederick had known Quantz since he was 16 years old. He had insisted on flute lessons despite his domineering father's wishes to the contrary.

"I guess," admitted Frederick, "our days tootling the flute are over. But we did have a good time though, didn't we?"

Frederick was 61 years old now, suffering from arthritis and gout. His technique had fallen off since that damned Seven Years' War which seemed to go on forever. Music stopped in Berlin when the army went off to war to repulse the Austrians and the British. The King had a few missing teeth which made it difficult to play his flute.

At least, Frederick's forces took Dresden away from the Polish King. That used to be Quantz' old patron and his home, until Quantz was seconded to Berlin through some diplomatic dealings in 1740. Quantz had played in Frederick's private chamber group. He rubbed shoulders with the likes of C.P.E. Bach and even earned a bigger salary than the younger Bach.

"I'm proud of what I've done in life," said Quantz breathing hard. "There must be 15 new compositions which I have not shown Your Majesty yet. They should be in the cupboard in my study too."

At this, Mme Quantz blinked. She had gone through Quantz' old study and packed the manuscripts and sent them off to a friend.

"We might make money out of this once Quantz dies," she had said.

Frederick asked, "15 new manuscripts?" Quantz nodded in agreement.

"Preserve them for posterity," said Quantz in a whisper. "Maybe there is a gifted young man who might enjoy them."

He repeated to Frederick that he had redesigned 6 new flutes. His Majesty was welcome to have them, whichever one he preferred for his old toothless mouth. They both briefly laughed.

"It helps to have teeth," joked his Majesty with a toothless grin.

"Yes, maybe some gifted young man might do a better service to your flutes than an aging, withered old monarch."

Frederick nodded to his valet who whispered in his ear. "Your Majesty, the drawer is empty. There were no manuscripts in it."

Frederick eyed the old crone, Mrs. Quantz, who stood in the corner looking blankly at the ceiling. Frederick said nothing, intending to solve the problem later of the missing manuscripts and the flutes. Frederick would interrogate Mrs. Quantz, but not now, not until old Quantz had gone to his heavenly rest. There must not be a scene in the house at the moment. Give the old flautist peace in his own home.

John Hartig   Two Baroque Prodigies

Frederick nodded at the valet who was not only a personal servant but also somewhat of an interrogator for Frederick.

Frederick said, "You have work to do...but later."

Quantz raised his head a bit off the pillow. The birds outside were still singing like a heavenly choir.

"I hear beautiful music," he said, "flutes are singing me to sleep."

Frederick held his old tutor's hand. He squeezed lightly. He said, "It's been a privilege, old master flautist."

"And with you, Your Majesty."

Quantz raised his head once again as the birds twittered on. He fell back with his last breath, dead. This was the day the music had died!

26
Missing Manuscripts

Frederick had agreed to pay Quantz 100 ducats for every hand-crafted flute he made. The King kept his promise and designated 600 ducats for 6 flutes to be given to the wife after this whole affair was sorted out. However, first the 15 manuscripts and 6 flutes had to be tracked down and recovered.

The valet set about his detective work to locate and get Quantz's missing materials back.

It was discovered that Mrs. Quantz had an affair with one of the lesser musicians in the Berlin orchestra. Through that connection, she had hoped to sell Quantz's manuscripts on the black market. "Surely, they must be worth some money," she said to herself.

Maybe, her violinist lover could network and get rid of the flutes and the manuscripts secretly. But the plan did not go well.

Quantz's compositions were specific to the flute and that in the 18th century was not marketable, except to the people who loved and played the flute privately. The new flutes might be worth something, but when the dealer in musical instruments saw the changes in design which Quantz had made, he did not understand their function. So, he said to Mrs. Quantz, "These are worthless. They aren't really flutes because of the extra keys on them."

Mrs. Quantz was in a quandary. What was an old widow to do?

John Hartig   Two Baroque Prodigies

The valet questioned her in a spare room at the King's Palace. The King was present, looking questioningly at the old woman.

"But Your Majesty," she pleaded, "what is an old widow to do in her old age?"

"I suppose," said Frederick, "live within your means?"

The valet entered the interrogation room with a short man, somewhat in disarray because he had been manhandled by the valet. The valet held a folder with a bunch of papers inside.

"The manuscripts your Majesty!" he said. "This little man is a violinist in your royal orchestra."

Frederick counted the compositions inside the folder. "Yes," he said, "15 of them. What about the flutes?"

"In storage in a music shop," said the valet. "We also have all 6 of them which we've confiscated."

When Frederick added these 6 to his other collection, accumulated over the years, as Quantz had refined his technique in crafting new flutes with better intonation, Frederick owned a total of 11 Quantz-made flutes.

The regent could have just seized the instruments for his own without payment because, once Quantz died, Frederick by agreement, owned everything that Quantz had ever produced, all his compositions and all his hand-crafted flutes.

Frederick hesitated a moment and then said to the valet, "Throw Frau Quantz and her friend in the dungeon."

He did not intend this decision to be permanent, but Mrs. Quantz had been more than petty and more than dishonest. She had no respect for her husband or for his great talent. Perhaps, some time in jail would teach them both a lesson.

The final decision, after conferring with his royal advisors, was that the violinist would be fired from his position in the royal orchestra. He was told to leave Berlin and seek his fortune elsewhere.

As to Mrs. Quantz, she received the monies that the King had promised to Quantz, since his employment to the King, 600 ducats for 6 flutes and bonuses for the 15 compositions which the King and his valet recovered. In this, he was more than generous.

Frederick was kind enough to provide the widow with a little apartment in Berlin for life. Before her release from jail, Frederick visited her and said, "Did you not think that Quantz was dear enough to me, that I would not have provided for his widow? I hope you have learned something from your experience."

Who knows if she became less greedy, less critical or a bit wiser through her treatment. She got a house out of the deal. However, she disappeared from the annals of history, fading into obscurity.

Frederick the Great asked himself, "How could Quantz ever have been so naïve as to marry her?" He had never heard the story about how the old widow had tricked poor old Quantz into marriage. Maybe, it was better that Frederick had never heard the story.

Frederick had a huge memorial erected outside the Nauener Tor in the Potsdam churchyard in memory of Quantz. A poor man's son who had risen high above his station in life!

27
Legacy

When I scoured through our local library for books on Johann Joachim Quantz, there were no books!

There was a fair bit on the internet in Google, but sadly nothing in print. After the brief mention that Quantz got married to Anna Rosina in 1737, there wasn't much about her married life to Quantz, except that she tricked him into marriage, and she hen-pecked the poor man. I found nothing on her later years or when she died. When I asked the librarian if she ever heard of Johann Joachim Quantz, she said, "No."

Even among modern flute players, Johann Joachim Quantz has a long way to go to be appreciated and rediscovered.

He was a highly successful musician during the Baroque Era, not only because of his actual talent but also because of his personal relationship with His Highness, King Frederick the Great of Prussia. Unfortunately, Quantz has been swept under the rug as the years have passed by.

Little of his repertoire has made it to modern times, because he was the private musical tutor to the King of Prussia, Frederick the Great. It is suggested that as the King's personal musician, this hampered Quantz' output as a composer and also his fame.

Kayla Low writes in her master thesis on Quantz, "While it certainly was not uncommon for composers to be in service of a powerful patron, Quantz's relationship with his employer has harmed Quantz's legacy to a greater extent than other contemporaneous composers." *[Low, ch3, p.41]*

He was a renowned flautist, composer, and author of an enduring treatise on performance practice. There are apparently seven portraits of the great musician, one of them unfortunately lost. The passing of years has relegated him to the background of musical history, so that not much is known of him. Very little was published of his works during his lifetime. Only a small portion is in print today.

Yet, during his lifetime, he had enormous status and earned an enormous salary. Perhaps, little is known of him because he concentrated his compositions mostly to the flute. Also, he sold his services exclusively to His Majesty, King Frederick II, and so he was overshadowed by His Majesty in history.

Johann Joachim Quantz should be looked on as the Stradivarius of flute making, despite the fact that the design of the flute became revolutionized by others after Quantz' death.

Quantz for his time did some amazing things in flute design. Certainly, someone like Theobald Boehm switched the design to the silver flute which in modern times is so popular. We even have James Galway today who is known as the man with the golden flute.

However, Quantz was a visionary during the Baroque Era. He was a pioneer. He invented the telescoping end-joint of the transverse flute, so that the flautist could change pitch a half a tone either way for fine tuning. *[Feike Bonnema, flute builder]*

Flutes still use that design today.

28
Popularizing Quantz

Modern flautists should promote the old master's repertoire. Unfortunately, much of his repertoire is still not categorized and played, hidden away and dormant in manuscript form in the library archives in Berlin.

It is hoped that this problem will be corrected by the pressure of young flute players and of the music programs at universities.

Kayla Ann Low admits, in her Master of Music thesis, that the lack of Quantz's repertoire is still too obviously missing in educational institutions. "The repeated appearance of Telemann on a competition program shows that he has been accepted into the flute's standard repertoire while a composer like Quantz has not." *[Low thesis, p.68]*

Low sees university music programs as playing a key role in bringing Quantz back. "Students at major universities with prominent flute programs eventually influence the trajectory of flute repertoire around the country as they become teachers themselves." She sees that their influence can make a difference to the resurgence of Quantz's material. *[Low thesis, p.75]*

Kayla Ann Low feels badly that Quantz is neglected, a talent who deserves much more recognition for his contributions to the design of the flute and to its repertoire. He should be treated better.

> Quantz simply does not get the same treatment as contemporaneous composers despite the magnitude of his contributions as seen through his treatise,

advancements of the instrument, and massive amount of compositional output. *[Low thesis, p.79]*

Johann Joachim Quantz wrote almost 300 flute concertos, 200 flute sonatas, 45 trio sonatas and 9 horn concertos. He also wrote chamber music for various instruments.

Some scholars judge that Quantz' book on the comprehensive guide to flute playing, the *Versuch* or *The Attempt*, was his greatest achievement. However, Quantz remained hidden in the wings because an English translation of his autobiography did not appear until 1951!

When Quantz died, all his manuscripts became property of the King. That is why they survived, and why we have copies of them. However, they ended up collecting dust in the library archives in Berlin, as previously mentioned.

Kayla Low looks at why Quantz has been neglected, overshadowed by others in the annals of music history. She acknowledges in her thesis, that, "Not much is written about Quantz from the period after the Seven Years' War as a consequence of spending his remaining years with an aging monarch." *[Low. p.45]* Those years must have been difficult on Quantz, the musical darling of His Majesty. Quantz was neglected in those warring years which withered the spirit of music in Berlin because the monarch had to attend to other matters of state, not matters of music.

The manuscript collections of Quantz and Frederick are stored at the *Sächsische Landesbibliothek* which is the State Library of Berlin. Since they are still in manuscript form, they are not ready for printing for the public. Works between the two men have become so entangled that musicologists would have a difficult time sorting them out.

After all, Frederick took over and stored Quantz' works mixed them up with his own, since as King, he owned Quantz' manuscripts outright. Even today, the number of Quantz' compositions are unknown. They are neither published nor dated. *[naxos.com]*

Quantz remained at the Prussian court in the service of Frederick the Great until his death in 1773. The King himself completed an unfinished sonata at the time of Quantz' death, an act which was a great tribute to Quantz, his mentor. Frederick had a huge memorial erected outside the Nauener Tor in the Potsdam churchyard in memory of Quantz.

Flute design changed over the next century without Quantz, and his old-style flutes are no longer used. It is said that there are only three people in all of Berlin who know how to play Quantz' old wooden flutes. Now, the silver flute is the modern standard! And the renowned modern flautist, James Galway, is "the man with the golden flute"!

Concerts of Quantz' works are held regularly in Scheden, his birthplace. His popularity is on the rise though, long overdue!

Sources

Wikepedia, Johann Joachim Quantz, article.

Wikipedia, Elisabeth Christine of Brunswick-Wolfenbuttel-Bevern, not to be confused with Elisabeth Christine Ulrike.

Wikipedia, *Hans Hermann von Katte*, portrait of young Frederick pleading for mercy before von Katte got beheaded.

Britannica, Frederick William I, King of Prussia.

New World Encyclopedia, "Johann Joachim Quantz", biography summary.

Boulezian, The King of Prussia: Frederick the Great and Opera, 2012.

Biography of Johann Joachim Quantz, 1697-1773, site publ. by Feike Bonnema, 1916.

Boulezian, The King of Prussia: Frederick the Great and Opera, 2012.

Elysium Ensemble, Johann Joachim Quantz, An Account of his life. Cites quotes from his autobiography. Talks about his European Tour and people he met.

Radio Swiss Classic, Music Database of Johann Joachim Quantz, from Wikipedia, ref. born as "Hanß", brief biography by dates.

The Sound, A Dictionary of Music and Musicians/ Quantz, Johann Joachim, article by Franz Gehring.

Wondrium Daily, Music History Monday: The Best Gig in the World! By Prof. Robert Grreenberg, Ph.D. article January 31, 2017.

Walkerhomeschoolblog, Johan Joaquim Quantz and his Flute Concerti, 2017.

Yumpu, Ed. J.A. Fuller Maitland, Grove's Dictionary of Music and Musicians, in Five Volumes, Macmillan Co., 1906. Seven years' war end of flute playing.

Charles Walthall, Portraits of Johann Joachim Quantz, November Edition of *Early Music*, 1986, p. 501.

Anja Weinberger, Johann Joachim Quantz, blog.

Ellen Elizabeth Exner, Dissertation: *King Frederick the Great and Music for Berlin*, 1732-1756, publ. 2010. Exner mentions Quantz several times among a bunch of other musicians who strengthened the royal court in Berlin to replace the acclaim of Dresden and the Polish court.

Kayla Ann Low, Dissertation for Master of Music, *Lost in Translation: The Largely Unknown Life and Contributions of Johann Joachim Quantz*, 2022. Detailed modern account of research on Quantz. Also argues for Quantz as a viable source for public performance in flute repertoire.

Rachel Brown, "Private passion: the sonatas by Johann Joachim Quantz

John Hartig   Two Baroque Prodigies

Kathryn Hadley article, History Today, Frederick the Great's Erotic Poem, publ. 2011.

Johann Joachim Quantz, On Playing the Flute, Buy book offer.

Albert Quantz on biography of Johann Joachim Quantz, the design of the flute. Quantz' fingering p. 233.

Andrea Kapell Loewy, *Frederick the Great: Flutist and Composer*, in College Music Symposium, Oct. 1990.

Meike ten Brink, Eng. Trans. By David Stevens, Johann Joachim Quantz, naxos.com.

John S.C. Abbott, *Frederick the Great*, Harper and Brothers, New York, 1871, avail. ebook through Gutenberg.org. Free use.

BOOK 2
Jean-Marie Leclair
1697-1764

A Baroque Violin Prodigy
The Unsolved Murder Mystery
of a Violinist and Composer

Copyright © John Hartig
First Edition 2019
Revised Edition 2024

John Hartig   Two Baroque Prodigies

Jean-Marie Leclair

Note: Leclair's violin was a Stradivarius made in 1721 in Cremona. It is called, "Le Noir", because of a black stain on it, which legend says was from Leclair's blood from a mortal stab wound as he lay dying in the vestibule of his house. The modern-day owner of this rare instrument is Italian conductor, Guido Rimonda, a modern violin virtuoso.

Synopsis

Jean-Marie Leclair was one of the best 18th century violinists. He was also a respected composer who, during the Baroque Era, rightfully earned the title of "the founder of the French school of violin".

Sadly, he was stabbed to death either on October 22nd late at night, or October 23rd early morning, in 1764, when it was still dark. His body was found in the vestibule of his home which was located on the seedy side of Paris. Leclair was 67 years old.

No one was ever accused or arrested in the case, despite strong suspicions. It could have been a nephew who was envious of Leclair's success with the violin, playing in King Louis XV's Orchestra. It could have been his ex-wife who made money out of publishing and printing his manuscripts. It could have been a collaboration by both of them, the nephew and the ex-wife, or it might even have been a deed committed by a fellow musician, Jean-Pierre Guignon. One other possibility must be entertained that the killing could have been done gratuitously by a break and enter criminal unknown by anyone because, after all, Leclair lived alone in a seedy part of town and frequented the pubs for drinks. Perhaps, Leclair's environment made the police dismiss the case without much follow-up. Besides detective work in those days was in its infancy and there was no support in what you call "the administration."

*****

This novella captures the atmosphere of the Baroque Era in which Jean-Marie lived, tracing his life, his successes and failures and uncovering the motive and the person or persons who might have done the cowardly deed of killing him. It's a shame that nothing was ever proved in the crime and that no arrests were ever made. Indeed, it's a shame that the crime ever happened at all, and that the world was deprived of such a great talent who might have had a few more compositions to give to the world.

It's a perplexing case. A cold case, lying dormant for over 250 years. What clues can this novella uncover which might crack the case? Who could have done it? Who killed Jean-Marie Leclair?

*****

Chapter 1

Coffeehouse Chatter
October 24, 1764

The usual crowd was drifting in: Denis Diderot, the Montgolfiers, Voltaire, even Leclair's old violin rival, Jean-Pierre Guignon, who was now collecting a pension for his long years of service in the Royal Symphony and the Royal Chapel. The King himself was not there. Word got around that Louis XV would at least be represented by his aide at the funeral.

Within the week and following months, news and gossip would spread among all the coffeehouses throughout Europe that Jean-Marie Leclair, once chief violinist and composer in the King's court, was dead. It would be a hot topic for some time, not because a talented man was dead, but rather because of how he was dead. Assassinated, they said, stabbed in the back three times!

The news was of course a perfect topic for coffeehouse discussion about how or why Jean-Marie Leclair was murdered. It was the sort of thing that titillated people. But the chatter would not last long in these gossip circles. After all, Leclair was only a minor luminary in the music world. His time had come and gone. He was already 67 when he was so callously murdered. Others, younger, were waiting in the wings. They had already been chomping at the bit to race out onto the musical stage. Leclair, in hindsight, had missed his chance to stay in the limelight.

During the height of his powers, he had been too proud to care about catering to Kings and Queens to ensure a name for himself in the annals of musical history. Then, as he aged, those younger, more agile and indeed, more talented, were shrewd enough to market their names and their fame through the cultivated patronage of Europe's Kings and Queens. The new luminaries in 1764 were Haydn at age 30, and an even younger, Amadeus Mozart, at the age of 8, beloved of God.

Voltaire clapped his hands to warm up as he came through the door of the historic Café de Procope, shivering out of the cold. Winter came early to Paris that year. It was bright and chilly that morning on October 24, 1764, giving thought to those who could afford it, to head south to their villas on the Côte d'Azur. Voltaire broke into a warm smile as he spotted his coffee companions. He held his chin imperiously high, hailing the waiter for his usual order of "le petit noir". He also asked for a slice of torte with his coffee.

He felt effusive, as if today were any different than any other day in which he felt effusive. "Did you hear about Leclair?" he asked. "The man was murdered last night, stabbed in the back. Whatever his ambitions in life, they now lie in the dust. He will no longer give us melodious Sonatas and Concerti with which to brighten our world. 'Dommage. Très dommage!'"

Voltaire sat down next to Diderot, laying out the details: "Yes, stabbed in the back, not once but three times! What a coward the culprit must be! He could at least have faced the man and done it from the front. The police are now seeking the felon who appears to have gotten clear away."

Diderot shook his head in sadness, "France has a lost a gem. I remember just last month discussing with him the value of my Encyclopedia, which is my ambition in life to collect all knowledge of all mankind in various volumes. I pray to Heaven to have enough time to finish this project. Jean-Marie Leclair asked me if there was a market for such a thing. But after a pause, he relented, saying he did see value in it, after all, for any man who wished to educate and improve himself. Leclair admitted to his own penchant for self-improvement, editing and then re-editing his musical scores until each note was weighed and placed so meticulously on his score that it became musical perfection. He confessed that he even burned some of his failed manuscripts because they were not good enough."

The Montgolfiers each sipped their strong coffee and munched thoughtfully on a piece of cake. They weighed their words carefully among these august and learned companions because compared to them they were only boys. They lived off the proceeds of their lucrative paper manufacturing business. Joseph-Michel was only 24 years old, and his brother, Jacques-Etienne, a mere 19. They gave deference to these older companions, but occasionally, drew up enough courage to have their say. Joseph-Michel asked, whether Leclair had been a nice man, or if he had enemies, or if indeed, he could be considered a gem in the coffers of France's musical legacy?

Jean-Pierre Guignon, once the King's premier violinist, offered his opinion, "Yes, Leclair was indeed talented, but he had an infuriating personality." Guignon recalled, "Back in 1734, the King gave him a gold-plated pocket watch, since Leclair had dedicated several compositions to him. Leclair had a habit of pulling out this watch at rehearsals and saying, 'I see, by the King's watch, that I have three more minutes to sit in my first violin chair before we commence rehearsal...or he would say, 'I see by the King's watch, that I have just enough time to get to my scheduled appointment with the King'."

Guignon continued his recollections of Leclair: "I admit he was an accomplished violinist, much like me, of course. We agreed that we would share the first violin position in the Royal Symphony and alternate that honour every month. He went first, but when it was my turn the following month, guess what the scoundrel did? He quit the symphony just so he would not have to take directions from me because he considered himself superior."

That was almost 30 years ago, and the resentment still smoldered in Guignon's heart. Guignon looked his companions fully in the eyes and affirmed, "I swear by heaven, however, that I did not kill the man for an old resentment. I've had a steady job in the King's employ all these years and have earned the respect of my fellow Parisians, playing first violin in the Royal Symphony and then in the Royal Chapel. I have been satisfied with my accomplishments, and now enjoy a good pension."

Guignon took a moment and finally commented that, with Leclair's instability and unreliability, history would soon forget the man. "Perhaps he will be remembered more for the way he died, than for the value of his works."

The Montgolfiers sipped some more coffee, took another bite out of their torte, and then, finally spoke to defend the dead man who could not be there himself. "You are speaking ill of the dead." said the younger brother. "Even if it were true, you should treat the man kindlier because he had the misfortune to die such a cruel death."

"Maybe France has indeed lost a gem," continued the older brother, "who is to say what Leclair might yet have added to our musical history?"

Voltaire cut in: "Maybe he would have added nothing, certainly judging from the way he was going." He chuckled cynically and added, "As usual, the Montgolfiers are full of hot air. Next you will make Leclair out to be a benign saint or a national hero. A gem indeed! You two need to stick to your ballooning. Perhaps you can see to it that mankind will indeed fly before the end of the century."

The older Montgolfier, Joseph-Michel, reposted: "That indeed is a challenge within our grasp, and we will make it so, mark my words. Do you not agree, little brother?" Jacques-Etienne nodded his head. The older Montgolfier continued, "I see us flying above Paris skies before the century is done...and that, dear Voltaire, is not hot air!" Voltaire's eyebrows lifted, admiring Joseph-Michel's spunk. He simply uttered, "I can hardly wait."

*****

The Montgolfiers were indeed successful in a piloted flight over Paris in 1783. That was 19 years after Voltaire's brazen challenge and Leclair's death.

The group enjoyed the exchange immensely and ordered another cup of "le petit noir". After a pause, Guignon asked, "So, who is going to the funeral tomorrow?"

He let the group know that the ceremony itself was to be at The Church of Saint-Laurent on the Ile-de-France.

"Burial will be right afterwards. I intend to make an appearance at least for the eulogy inside the church. But I don't want to stand out in the cold for the burial."

Everyone agreed: "The ceremony it is then," Voltaire agreed, suggesting that everyone meet back at Procope's Café afterwards in order to warm up with a lovely slice of cake and coffee. "You know," he said in reflection, "If France were ever to go to war again, it would have to be with coffee and cake served at the front."

Chapter 2

The Funeral
Ile-de-France, Church of Saint-Laurent
October 25, 1764

The church was huge, ornamented with spires and great columns. Large stained-glass windows let in colourful light. The massive structure, like all the beautiful cathedrals in Paris, was paid for by weekly donations from the coins of the poor, as well as the more lucrative gifts from the nobility of Paris. The incentive to pay for those great churches which reached the skies to praise God or aspire to man's ambitions was incited by the fiery tongues of priests who said that the passageway to heaven was secured by how much money you gave to the church.

On the morning of October 25, 1764, the attendance inside the church was sparse. One might say that this was a sign that Leclair had very few friends, if indeed any. The coffeehouse group was there, the family, and the ex-family. Yes, there were indeed a few so-called friends there, as well as Leclair's former landlord, Monsieur Legras. The King's coach pulled up to the front entrance, the coat of arms, boldly displayed on the doors of the coach. Louis XV's aide stepped out, meeting the priest at the door with his regrets from the King who was elsewhere attending to other matters of State.

Despite the cold, a cold which bit the skin, some comfort came from the fact that the sun shone brightly down upon this sad occasion. The King's aide slipped an envelope [full of money] into the priest's hand, whispering, "With the King's condolences and gratitude".

Inside the church, the sun also had an amazing effect through the stained-glass windows so that people's faces were bathed in a myriad of soft colours. Radiance and iridescence shone above the head of Jesus. While the attendees stared at the stained-glass windows and at the streaks of light coming in, they concentrated on the demise of the deceased in quiet whispers of gossip.

Voltaire couldn't resist. He leaned over to Guignon in the pew and remarked. "We've got to stop meeting like this." Only a month previously, Rameau had passed away in early September, just 13 days shy of his 81st birthday. That timing surely eclipsed the news of Leclair's untimely death. Voltaire added as an after-thought, "Leclair's murderer could have at least had the decency to kill the man later, so as to give Leclair a chance to enjoy fully the sole announcement of his untimely death."

Guignon remarked, "I was at Rameau's funeral only last month at St. Eustache. He was a strange one, an old man truly cantankerous. Irascible, critical and generally hard to get along with. Maybe all geniuses are that way?"

"Not me!" countered Voltaire with a self-indulgent smile.

"Well, he was irksome anyway, and a miser too. They found a bag full of 'Louis d'or' gold coins in his room. Maybe he thought he could take it with him! Bribe Saint Peter at the Pearly Gates, you know, like the Catholic Church seems to practice with their indulgences." Both men chuckled. Voltaire said, "All this heavenly bribery does not concern me. I am a devout atheist. Besides if there is a God, I would not believe in the same God as the Catholic Church." Guignon was pleased, "Ah, an atheist after my own heart, but I admit, there is something to be said for ritual and religious ceremony in society?"

John Hartig   Two Baroque Prodigies

The priest was not amused with all this chattering in the pews, which to his ears sounded like the buzzing of bees. He harrumphed and asked for respectful silence. "Let us have kindly reflection and forgiving thoughts about the departed soul," he announced, and he bowed his head. No one spoke. The crowd seemed to sink into a pensive mood more appropriate to this somber occasion of a great composer's passing.

Jean-Marie Leclair, at one time, had been one of the most famous violinists and composers in all of France. No one knew who had killed him. What coward had stabbed the man in the back three times? What were the police doing to catch the culprit? Jean-Marie Leclair was only 67 years old. Who knows what other great works he could have written for posterity?

The priest highlighted Jean-Marie Leclair's accomplishments. He called him the "French Corelli" and the "French Bach". The priest pointed out the wide range of Leclair's talents, starting out as a ballet dancer; and later pursuing a career as a virtuoso violinist, and finally, making a name for himself as a composer. Leclair wrote numerous Violin Sonatas for one and two violins, Trios, Violin Concertos, and one opera, *Scylla et Glaucus*, a tragedy in five acts.

The priest's Eulogy briefly touched on all these points, as if these praises were prayers raised to God to allow Leclair straightaway into Heaven for the excellence of his accomplishments. The Eulogy was closed with an appropriate mention of the King, "The King sends his condolences and his apology that he could not be here, attending to other matters of State."

Shortly, some men in the church got up and headed toward the coffin, grasping its handles and then ceremoniously marching their burden outside into the churchyard where the hole had been dug, open and gaping, waiting to take in Jean-Marie's earthly remains. The ceremony was short and sweet, thankfully short, because it was so cold outside. The priest blessed the casket, sprinkled holy water on it, and then the coffin was lowered into the ground. Nobody threw flowers in, or any scoopfuls of dirt. They were eager to get to Le Procope and get warm.

At least the great musician left physical evidence of his work outside the grave to show the world that he had actually lived and created something in his sheet music. Jean-Marie Leclair left behind printed copies of many Sonatas and Concerti, which were reprinted in many libraries around the world. But how many times were they played and praised? That question was held at the mercy of an uncertain posterity and the hazards and the trends and changing tastes of time.

Meanwhile, the former landlord, Legras, schemed about how he could get the title back to the little house on the Rue Careme-Prenant, so that he could resell it. He had done well with Leclair/ He sold the unit twice reeking in a good profit, since Leclair was desperate to get away from his wife. Ah, a wife, the jewel in your crown, or the stone! Maybe that aspect of marriage was either luck or fate! Monsieur Legras wondered whom he could line up next to flip his house to in that disreputable part of "le Marais". The ex-wife wondered if there were any other extant manuscripts left in the house, which she could get her hands on, so her engraving company could print them and she could make a profit from her dead husband.

Clear sunlight shone on the very tiny group huddled around the plot of dirt outside the old church. The coffeehouse companions had already filtered away. Sunlight almost seemed to bless the remaining few who stood in silence around the grave. The priest nodded to those few who remained, that they were dismissed.

That left only the grave diggers with the priest, waiting for his other nod to proceed with the drudgery of shoveling dirt into the grave. The priest left.

The gravediggers were alone with their work, eager to get it done and get out of the cold. Bruno hesitated, "Now that the priest is gone, what about digging the grave up again and checking Leclair out for valuables. Maybe a ring or a watch? Maybe his violin is in there?" Jacques was none too keen.

"Earlier today, I visited my old friend the coroner. Leclair lay naked as a jaybird on the table. I rifled through all his clothes. No rings, no watches, nothing! I heard that the violin was smashed at the neck by the killer, so there is nothing to take away, if we dig up the grave again."

Bruno looked disconsolate. Jacques said, "There's nothing for it old buddy, but get the work done here before we get drowned in the grave with the downpour that I see coming from the east."

They kept up a routine shoveling dirt into the grave, periodically tamping it down with their big boots, and then adding another layer of dirt with the objective to bring the grave to ground level before the big downpour. When they were at the top, they patted down the loose earth above Jean-Marie Leclair with the flat of their shovels, so that he would be secure until the second coming of Christ.

"Don't worry about tromping the dirt down too hard and loudly," said one grave digger to the other, "he can't hear us anyway. He's deaf." They laughed.

All in all, it had been a lovely October day, though nippy. A hint of clouds was blowing in from the East which threatened to make the air even colder and more biting.

The Procope coffee klatch were more than relieved to get back into the warmth of the Café and back to the comfort of a nice slice of torte and a hot cup of "le petit noir".

"We have good topics to discuss," commented Voltaire. "Death and dying, God and eternity, and oh yes, our very troubled Catholic Church," he said.

Chapter 3

The Crime Scene
October 23, 1764

Jacques Paysant, the gardener, was walking to the house in the early morning of October 23rd to pull some dying shrubbery on that fateful day of Jean-Marie's death. The first bite of an early winter was in the air. As the worker came up the walk, he saw something suspicious in the vestibule of the little house. The front door was open, and a man's boots were sticking out. The gardener cautiously got closer and realized the full importance of what he was seeing, his employer lying face down within the vestibule. The man's white wig lay disheveled and somewhat dislodged off the man's head. Paysant realized that his employer was stone-dead. Strangely enough, his first thought was not about the horror of the scene, but about how to clean the man's wig? There was blood on it. "Now it's ruined!"

Over the past six years, Paysant had held this part-time job here at Leclair's little house on the Rue Careme-Prenant. He was used to seeing Leclair take little walks, adorned with a white wig, a fashion of distinction for the gentry of the time. Paysant had seen many men with wigs come and go from the little house over the years, because after all, his employer was still a respected musician in Paris. But the gardener kept his opinion about wigs to himself and gave deference to these lofty visitors whenever they graced the doorway of Leclair's little home. Paysant privately sneered at them behind their backs because they assumed a haughty air as if style truly made the man.

Powdered wigs became fashionable when Louis XIII first wore one back in 1624 to hide his baldness. Before long, the perruque was all the rage among the upper-and middle-class men in Europe, as a fashion statement, and not just to hide a receding or graying hairline. Men of quality in 18th century Europe lined up like peacocks to distinguish themselves as a superior class from the working poor like the gardener. Styles and length of wigs even mirrored the level of society among nobles and people of culture.

Paysant pictured how absolutely ridiculous this trend was. He would never wear a wig to work, where his curly hairdo would get caught in the vines and shrubbery of his daily chores in the garden. He often chuckled at the outrageous thought of himself in a wig. His employer, of course, wore a perruque because of his higher station in life, and his distinction as a composer and a virtuoso violinist. Well, thought the gardener, "I suppose the man has earned the right to wear a wig. He is educated and has talent. And he is respected and recognized in society. I'll grant him that."

But if it came to hard labour with his fingers, Leclair would always say, "Let the gardener do it." The gardener harbored a private attitude of reverse superiority though, sneering down at his betters behind their backs. Openly, Paysant dared not show his disrespect. After all, this was 18th century France, and one must accept one's station and not mock one's betters.

Paysant snapped his attention away from the bloody wig. He took another cautious step towards the opened door. A few miscellaneous objects lay strewn about around Leclair's body, within the vestibule, a book of some sort and a musical script not far from the man's hand. Paysant saw the nasty stab wounds in and around the man's neck, three of them, glistening dark and wet. He asked two questions: Who did this? And why? He shook his head in disbelief, backtracked and called for help. His work for the day was done!

Instead of his neck, some sources have said Leclair's stab wounds were in the back. The point was that Leclair was dead!

Three police officers were assigned to the case: the Lieutenant of Police, Antoine-Gabriel de Sartine, and two lower-level policemen, Monsieur Gentilhomme and Monsieur Lebrusque. They concluded that the assault happened either during the night of October 22nd or sometime in the early morning of October 23rd when it was still dark. "Maybe we'll never find the killer," said one of the officers with discouragement.

Unfortunately, the murder weapon was missing. That might have been a key piece of evidence for tracking down the owner. But then, The Lieutenant of Police, Antoine-Gabriel de Sartine, knew that things were never simple in solving murder cases. "How inconsiderate of the culprit," he thought, "of the killer not to leave us the murder weapon!"

Budgets had always been a tight problem for the police in Paris, probably everywhere in Franc. Money! Money was also used to bribe police officers because the Parisian system was corrupt. De Sartine at least was a man of honour, and the men under him respected the man and loved working for him. The members of the "Garde" were mostly soldiers from the provinces, and had little loyalty to Paris itself, but they did have loyalty to someone like de Sartine. Strict, fair and respected!

Once you got to be a sergeant of the "Guet Royal", you got to wear the blue "justaucorps" which was a tight-fitting jacket with silver lace, a white feather in the hat, and red stockings, while the ordinary soldiers wore gray with brass buttons, red on their sleeve, and a jaunty feather in the hat and a bandolier, as part of the uniform. The feather in the cap made you feel special.

Both Gentilhomme and Lebrusque were sergeants, wearing police blue. They took some pride in that. By 1750, there were 19 posts of the Guet in Paris, each post manned by 12 guards. Their uniforms gave them clearances to scenes of a crime, and people got out of their way. Police responsibilities up to this point included monitoring bread prices, keeping traffic moving in the crowded streets, settling disputes, maintaining public order, chasing robbers and muggers...and of course, arresting murderers.

When the three officers went to the house, they had no trouble gaining access. The vestibule door was already open, and the interior door had been smashed. The former landlord met them there "in case they needed to be shown around". He had heard from somebody who had heard from somebody what had happened here, probably the gardener's grapevine. The landlord, or former landlord, was not just snoopy. He hovered around the premises with the hopes of getting his house back so he could resell it. Leclair and he had an agreement that Monsieur Legras had access to the house in case anything ever needed fixing. Leclair disdained physical labour and preferred paying somebody a couple of "livres" to use hammer and nail. When he first moved in, the roof leaked, and later shelves were required to be built in his study to store his precious manuscripts.

"Lieutenant," asked Gentilhomme, "do you think the landlord could have done it?"

The Lieutenant of Police answered, "Even though the man is greedy, he looks too dumb to do this kind of thing."

So, the three officers looked around, checking out the walkway and the vestibule which was blocked by the body. They skirted around Monsieur Leclair and entered the house. Lieutenant de Sartine noticed the bowl with coins in it, in plain view on top of an escritoire, or small desk, by the inside doorway. "Interesting," he thought, filing its significance away in his memory.

He walked to the bedroom and ventured to peek under the bed. He saw the chamber pot under there. It smelled. "Gentilhomme," he called, "why don't you take this thing outside. I saw a shovel in the backyard. Why don't you bury the contents at the back in a corner somewhere? Leave the chamber pot outside for M. Legras, to dispose of."

Gentilhomme wrinkled his nose at the chore, obediently stooping down to retrieve the chamber pot, which was unfortunately full. "Are you sure this isn't evidence?" commented Gentilhomme holding his nose. This only gained him a frown from his superior.

After some searching, the Lieutenant steepled his hands and puckered his lips in deep thought, "It appears that theft was not the motive here. We also found a bag of money under the mattress, and when we scrutinized the shelves in the study, all the man's manuscripts seemed to be intact. The violin was broken at the neck and the bow snapped in half, both lying on top of the harpsichord. That indicated obvious rage. The harpsichord itself is untouched. Other things indoors do not seem to be disturbed."

The Lieutenant commented, "Leclair lived simply but was not poor. His dwelling place here in Le Marais seemed to be a deliberate lifestyle." He asked himself why this was so. "For the life of me, I cannot understand why a man of modest means would prefer to live this way, here in this hovel, in the northern part of 'Le Marais', in a part of Paris that everyone knows is dirty and dangerous."

Lebrusque, the next officer in line [with some brains to his credit] offered an opinion. "Well, maybe the man was a recluse or a bit of a miser, living a bohemian lifestyle, determined to live without ostentation. He seemed to live frugally like a monk." The Lieutenant nodded. "Strangely enough, that makes sense. Lebrusque, when you're right, you're right!"

Gentilhomme remained silent, open-eyed like a blinking owl in a dark corner. He was merely the "yes man" in the group, a nice fellow enough, but one who did as he was told. "Someday, he will go far in the bureaucracy," thought Lieutenant de Sardine.

They had gone through everything in the house and came up with nothing. No real evidence, nothing that the murderer left behind. "It appears this was a pure crime of passion," said the Lieutenant finally, "Perhaps revenge or envy. The violin broken at the neck and the shattered violin bow speak volumes."

Lieutenant de Sardine had two other officers stand by with a coach from the coroner. They lifted the body into the coach and drove off, after de Sartine had one more quick inspection of the walkway, the wounds and the vestibule where the book and manuscript had been dropped. He wished that someday whatever the killer touched in the house could be used to find the killer. "Maybe such evidence will be useful someday but that someday is not now," said de Sartine dismissively to himself. He told the landlord that the scene must not be touched, and the house is not to be entered. He might have to come back next day for another inspection.

Chapter 4

The Police

Antoine-Gabriel de Sartine and the two sergeants went back to the police headquarters to discuss the facts. At that time, the police headquarters was called the Maréchaussée, not the Gendarmerie, which came later during Napoleon's time. De Sartine invited the two sergeants into his office. He sat behind his desk with steepled hands in serious concentration. The two sergeants sat on chairs facing their boss. De Sartine took a deep breath before he outlined the facts of the case as he saw them, and the plan of attack. He lit his pipe. He asked Sergeant Gentilhomme to take notes and make a list.

"Here are our suspects so far," he said. "We must start with the people who are readily available to us, and then there are those who, of course, are unknown, like a prowler or a hidden mistress." De Sartine drew on his long years of experience in the city's police force.

- first, there is the gardener, Jacques Paysant, who discovered the body
- it could be that one of Leclair's brothers, did the deed. They also were musicians,
- Leclair's own 40-year-old nephew, Guillaume-François Vial, son of Leclair's sister, Françoise, was a very likely suspect. He aspired to becoming a great violinist like his uncle who refused to promote the young man's career, and this sparked jealousy

- the ex-wife, Louise Roussel, made a good candidate. She owned the engraving business which made money out of printing Leclair's musical scores. Apparently, the business had come on hard times lately since Leclair and she divorced.
- then there is the possibility of a "rôdeur", a prowler who did Leclair in, though with the viciousness of the stabbing, a personal vendetta was more likely
- lastly, it could have been an angry mistress or a prostitute though this is doubtful because of the brute force of the stabbing. If it were a female, she could have hired a man to do the dirty work, which of course, would make the investigation more complicated?

"We have our work cut out for us," commented de Sartine. "We may never know who our killer is. We don't have the murder weapon. We do have perhaps two clues left at the house." De Sartine hesitated and puffed on his pipe, blowing out smoke that drifted leisurely to the ceiling like his thoughts. He asked, "Are you taking notes, Gentilhomme?" The sergeant fidgeted with his notepad, "Yes, Lieutenant, I have jotted down points as we go, for you to review later."

"So," continued the Lieutenant, "Whoever it was who broke through the inside door to gain access went in to look for something, but what? Theft seems unlikely since there were coins left so obviously in a bowl on the small desk, and of course, under the mattress. What is interesting, however, is that Leclair's violin lay broken at the neck on top of the harpsichord, as was the bow snapped in half. The harpsichord itself seemed untouched."

The Lieutenant continued to puff on his pipe, "It was rage that did this, rage aimed at Leclair and his most prized possession, the violin. Our killer did away with both, the violin and Leclair himself. Who would be so angry with the man? We saw that the man's books and manuscripts were still neatly stacked on the shelves in his study. Even the book and the manuscript he dropped when he was killed were left at the scene, though somewhat stained with blood."

"Are you taking notes, Gentilhomme?" asked the Lieutenant of Police. "Yes, yes, Lieutenant de Sartine. Every word." Although he did not mean every word, except point form and only the barest minimum. It didn't matter anyway because the record of Leclair's broken violin and his shattered bow never made it past the French Revolution. Gentilhomme's meticulous note taking went up in smoke as the citizens of Paris stormed government buildings, emptying desks, drawers and burning any papers they could find in 1789.

De Sartine expelled another puff of smoke. With finality, he said, "So, let's see what we can do about finding our killer! Lebrusque, have you brought in the gardener for our first interview?"

"Yes, Lieutenant de Sartine, the man is waiting ready for questioning."

"Let's get to it!" said the Lieutenant dismissively.
Jacques Paysant, the gardener, was escorted into a little room at the Maréchaussée. He was a big oaf of a man, a beefy peasant with a little head and small piggy eyes. He looked and acted dim. He entered the interview room hat in hand trembling. Officer Lebrusque equaled Paysant in stature, and stood within the small interview room, intimidating the gardener with his own big size. Lieutenant

de Sartine directed the proceedings quietly. Gentilhomme was asked and said yes to note-taking.

"Why would I kill my employer?" objected Paysant. "He was my source of income and he always paid me on time. I would not kill my own living." The Lieutenant saw the logic in this and with confidence made the interview short. "We are merely doing our jobs," said the Lieutenant, "I'm sorry this happened to your employer. It appears you have lost not only your employer but also some of your income. Your protestation is duly noted, however. Make a note of that Officer Gentilhomme."

"Yes sir," said the officer, as he scribbled away. "By the way, are you left-handed or right-handed?" asked de Sartine. "Right-handed," responded Paysant.

The Lieutenant cautioned Paysant, "We will let you go for now, but please, stay in Paris where we can reach you if we need to get more details." Paysant bowed his head in acknowledgement and was glad to get out of there with hat in hand. He was already known to the police at the headquarters after being brought in for several brawls at the La Dame Chantante, his favourite tavern. After he left the Maréchaussée, a sudden thirst hit him. He needed a drink.

"We have him on record," said de Sartine. "He has a habit of dropping into our building on a regular basis for matters of minor misdemeanors, basically drunkenness and brawls. Well, what do you think Sgt. Gentilhomme?"

"Yes sir," agreed the Sgt. most readily. "He likes his drink alright and his fights, and once he has a glass or two of wine, if he is our man, then he might just want to brag about it to his companions. We will keep an eye on him. I already sent the word out to our informants at La Dame Chantante and other taverns around the city, just in case he has a loose tongue."

"The only thing I see that the gardener has going for him," said the Lieutenant, "is that he is the one who brought the crime to our attention. I don't think the man is clever enough to stab his employer in the back and then cover the crime up by calling the police. That just brings attention to himself. He is also right-handed, and the attack was apparently carried out by a left-handed man."

De Sartine pointed out that the burly gardener easily had the physical power to dispatch his employer, with three vicious strokes to the upper back and neck. "The first blow," said the Lieutenant, "was delivered from behind, smashing the upper clavicle in two, close to the neck. This incapacitated Leclair, and already put an end to the man's violin playing career. The second blow came in at the side of the neck, severing the man's aorta. There must have been arterial spray everywhere, as is evidenced by the drenched book and manuscript of music which Leclair had in his hands. Then the third blow almost severed the man's spinal cord just below the neck. I don't think Leclair died instantly but it must have been a horrific realization for him to be dying."

The Lieutenant told his officers that Leclair was probably turned over immediately after the assassination. "It could have been that the killer shared a few words with Leclair face to face before the man died, and after that, the assassin turned Leclair back over again onto his stomach and dragged him into the vestibule to hide the body. The criminal was even fastidious enough to grab the book and manuscript from the walkway and throw those into the vestibule, as well. "

"And how do you know all that," asked Sgt. Gentilhomme, not wanting to be left in the dark. "Because there was a big pool of blood on the walkway and a smear that ran into the vestibule. The way I see it, the victim fell face down on the walkway, and then was turned over on his back bleeding profusely from his wounds in the upper back and neck." "Brilliant deduction," said Sgt. Gentilhomme. He was forever willing to ingratiate himself with his superior, whereas Sgt. Lebrusque shrugged his shoulders, not bothering to think in "deductions".

The Lieutenant continued, "There must have been immense strength in these blows, perhaps fueled by sheer anger. The gardener certainly had the strength, but a woman generally would not be capable of digging a knife so deeply into a man's neck. And then to drag the body into the vestibule to hide it until morning! If it was the ex-wife or a mistress, then she must have hired some man, which would make our case more complicated."

At the end of these speculations, the Lieutenant said, "I think our gardener, however, must remain on the list, just in case, and must remain available for further questioning." He added, "After all, the gardener has been imprisoned twice before. He is a recidivist. I am not happy with his testimony about when exactly he discovered the body, and where he was the night before."

"Uh, Lieutenant de Sartine, what's a recidivist?" asked Gentilhomme.

"Why, a convicted criminal who keeps doing the same old crimes," said the Lieutenant.

"Then, I guess I'm a recidivist," confessed Gentilhomme. "I come home every night and head straight-away to the tavern for a game of billiards with my buddies and a cup of wine."

"What does your wife say to that?" asked the Lieutenant.

"She said, I'll never change." They all laughed. At least, Gentilhomme wasn't a convicted criminal; just a policeman needing an outlet after a hard day's work. He liked his vices, and for all three officers, those were acceptable faults, not crimes. Their vices made their jobs as police officers bearable and sane; otherwise, there would have been no release from stress, and who knows, without that, they might have become criminals.

De Sartine sadly reflected on Leclair's demise, "Right from the first blow, Leclair's violin career was over. The man would never recover full mobility. What a tragedy for all those years of practice. A unique talent utterly destroyed." Gentilhomme scribbled more notes into his book as his superior ranged freely over his thoughts, openly and out loud, so that a written record of every detail could be kept on file. Gentilhomme had such neat handwriting, and he was meticulous in his notetaking.

Lebrusque was eager to get on with the investigation. "Sir, the Leclair siblings are next on our list. Three of them are also accomplished musicians. I have procured the use of several rooms for these interviews to keep these men separate."

"Then let us proceed," said the Lieutenant. He gestured towards Gentilhomme with a sign to bring his scribbling pad along.

Lebrusque pointed out to his superior that there were actually two Jean-Marie Leclairs, the older brother, called "l'aîné", because he was older, and Jean-Marie Leclair, the younger, called "le frère cadet". The older Leclair was 67 at his death, and the younger brother was 61 years old at that time. Despite their age difference, the brothers had been getting along quite well together, always had been since childhood.

Jean-Marie Leclair, the younger, was born in 1703, 6 years younger than his older namesake. After his brother was murdered, he outlived his older namesake by 13 years, reaching the venerable age of 80 at the time of his own death in 1777, which, was still not bad when the average life expectancy for a man in the 18th century was 41 years of age. Perhaps "le frère cadet" was a likely suspect because he seemed more competitive than the other brothers, and in fact, did achieve some minor success in a musical career, publishing a few meager pieces for two violins and one vocal piece of no account.

"Why should I be jealous?" challenged Leclair, the younger. "I loved my brother.
He was the other half of my soul. We played duets together when we were children." Jean-Marie Leclair, the younger, looked uncannily like a copy of his dead brother, similar build, and similar face. "I always admired my older brother," he swore, "and in fact, that goes for all my other brothers too."

The other two brothers pretty well said the same thing about each other. Pierre Leclair was 55. Benoit Leclair was 50. They loved the older Leclair and aspired to be better musicians because of him. "He was our inspiration; he gave us a goal," said Pierre. "He was my big brother; we looked up to him," said Benoit. When the interviews were over, the Lieutenant looked at each of his officers and shrugged his shoulders. "Who could argue with such a role model?" he said. Both Lebrusque and Gentilhomme agreed because they each had their own brothers, with whom they admittedly fought, but whom they dearly loved anyway. Whenever one of them got into a scrap around the neighbourhood, the other ones would bail them out. That was blood relations and what it meant to have family loyalty.

"We've interviewed the gardener and the brothers, so far," said de Sartine, "I will dismiss the gardener for now, for being too stupid, unless he spills something in the tavern other than his wine. Besides he is right-handed. Likewise, I will dismiss the three brothers for loving the deceased brother too much. Blood among brothers is thicker than water, and we will respect that, for the moment. They are also all right-handed."

Gentilhomme flipped his notebook. "Next on the list we have Guillaume-Francois Vial. He is Leclair's 40-year-old nephew, reportedly jealous of his virtuoso uncle and resentful that his uncle did not promote the nephew's career." "Ah," said de Sartine. "Nepotism, or rather the lack of it. No support for a slack nephew who never was a favourite of Leclair's anyway. Pure and simple. We have motive here, and possibly an opportunity if Vial was in the city for those two days during which the crime was committed."

When the nephew was called in the next day for the interview, all three officers were amazed at Vial's size, a huge man with enough apparent strength to plunge a knife deeply into any man's neck. The nephew's face looked young and innocent despite his 40 years. But he stood large and tall, 6' 4", with a broad back. The Lieutenant was impressed, thinking to himself, "I suppose not all violinists are the artsy and delicate type!" He also wondered how a violinist with a penchant for fine notes could find himself in such a massive body capable of extreme violence. The Lieutenant raised his eyebrows, and silently wondered, "And this is a violinist?" He judged that only the gardener and possibly Sgt. Lebrusque were equal to this man's huge stature and strength. How could such largeness be capable of touching the heartstrings of the soul with the mellifluous tones of a violin? Here stood one large contradiction. A giant who had a sweet gift, and as the police shortly found out, a foul mouth. Vial also insulted the nose, since he smelled badly.

John Hartig   Two Baroque Prodigies

He could have left his body odor outside the door of the small interrogation room. All three officers smelled it. "Worse even than our Superintendent!" thought de Sartine. Body odor was a commonplace occurrence during Leclair's lifetime and was generally accepted within reason and covered up with a good splash of cologne.

Everybody covered up their smells with other smells in those days, using perfumes and powders. Full body bathing was not practiced because it was a luxury. Plumbing and servants carrying water buckets cost money. Also, a belief was common that bathing in warm water was not healthy because it opened up the pores which let disease in. A moneyed household would install a scented fountain for their dinner parties or supplied each room with a "smelling box" that contained a sponge soaked in vinegar-based fragrances which masked the unpleasant odors emanating from the city streets. Maybe the only good thing that came out of this era was that France soon dominated the international perfume industry.

*****

After the initial shock of the man's size and smell, the officers soon faced another contradictory shock, the minute that Vial opened his mouth. There was no sweetness and light in his words, only a torrent of acerbic fluency of cursing, the mastery of which surprised even these seasoned officers of the police. Perhaps the production of sweet melodies and a gentle soul did not necessarily go together.

Vial let loose a string of invectives which expressed strong objections to being here at the Maréchaussée headquarters for questioning, questioning about something Vial absolutely and categorically denied. How dare they! Several other invectives pursued the first

When the man finally settled down, Lieutenant de Sartine said, "Well sir, welcome to police headquarters. These are my fellow officers, Sergeants Gentilhomme and Lebrusque. We would like you to have a seat!"

Chapter 5

November 2, 1764

The officers had a prearranged system. Good cop, bad cop. Gentilhomme was the good cop, looking innocent enough with his notepad. Lebrusque was the bad cop, using his big size and stern demeanor to intimidate. Lieutenant de Sartine was the referee.

"Reports tell us that you did not get along with your uncle. Why was that?" asked Lebrusque.

"It was obvious," said Vial with a sneer. "The old fellow did not give me a letter of introduction to the King's court, confirming that I was a gifted musician quite capable of playing both first and second violin in the Royal Symphony. I am a man of some considerable talent, you know!"

"The lack of a recommendation. Is that why you killed your uncle?" asked Lebrusque.

"Certainly not!" objected Vial, standing up as if slapped. A gentle hand from Officer Gentilhomme guided Vial back down into his seat. Lebrusque on the other hand preferred grabbing Vial and straightaway beating a confession out of the man. But as he had been often told before, by his stern minded superior, "We simply cannot do that. We need to be professional. This is 1764, after all!"

Vial looked convincing, "No, I swear that I did not lay a hand on my uncle. His endorsement could have meant the world to me. Why would I kill my ticket into the King's court?"

"Had you ever laid a hand on your uncle before?" pursued Lebrusque.

"Well, maybe there was that one time when I grabbed him by the lapel. He turned his back on me and said that my playing was at best mediocre. He called my talent minimal, and that I should practice for hours like he did when he was young."

"Perhaps, he was right. Practice makes perfect," commented Lebrusque. "But then what do I know about music, though I do know about hard work."

Lieutenant de Sartine cut in. "You are a healthy man, and I imagine, you like your drink and your women. Did you not frequent the taverns, especially La Dame Chantante?"

"Yes, I like a drink now and then," admitted Vial.

"And what about women? Instead of sawing away at your fiddle at home like a good boy to get your uncle's approval," asked Lebrusque.

"Now hear!" countered Vial. "Before you accuse me of the easy life, you need to look at my uncle's habits. He frequented prostitutes and had a mistress after the divorce from his wife. Maybe you need to look into that, and maybe that is the cause of his untimely death, not me!"

"Duly noted," said de Sartine nodding at Gentilhomme. "Make a note of that." "Yes sir," said Gentilhomme.

"Where were you on the night of October 22nd and the early morning of October 23rd?" asked Lebrusque.

"Why, probably at my usual haunt, La Dame Chantante, on the 22nd until the early morning, and then I rented a coach home because, as you know, the streets are unsavory during those hours in the early morning walking home alone. I slept it off until noon the next day, had a little lunch and then practiced my violin diligently until mid-afternoon."

"Sgt. Gentilhomme," commanded the Lieutenant, "Make a note so we can check his alibi out at a later date." Gentilhomme made a note.

The Lieutenant advised Vial not to leave Paris, in case there were further questions. "Do not fly south like the birds unless we issue a warrant for your arrest. By the way, are you right-handed or left-handed?"

Vial was confused, "why, I am ambidextrous. I am a very talented man, you know."

Lieutenant de Sartine lifted his eyebrows toward Gentilhomme to make a note of that. He said then to Vial dismissively, "You may go."

Vial rose with obvious disdain for the local constabulary. "Why don't you look at the ex-wife instead, or the mistress," he shot back in response.

When the unpleasant nephew was gone, all three officers wiped their brows in relief, and let out a sigh. "Well, good riddance to bad smells," said Lebrusque.

De Sartine complimented his team. "Good work," he said. "Perhaps, Guillaume-François would have trouble in the King's Symphony not only because of his personality but also because sitting beside him would be unbearably smelly."

Lebrusque commented, "He is some piece of work, and is so full of himself that he obviously over-estimates his own abilities."

"Aren't we all somewhat like that?" judged Gentilhomme. The other two officers smiled.

"Now let's line up the ex-wife for a little chat," said the Lieutenant. "However, if we are to do good police work, we need to do a background check on all our suspects. Why don't we grab some of our city records and bring them over to the Café de Procope, in more conducive surroundings, over a pleasant cup of coffee and a slice of cake. Wouldn't you agree our work would be more palatable there?" Needless to say, Gentilhomme and Lebrusque liked their boss. He had such good ideas.

Gentilhomme, as the "Yes Man", was the one who carried a box of files into the Café de Procope. De Sartine looked for a corner table where they could spread their work out, and sip coffee quietly, while they sorted through the files and solidified facts in their heads. Lebrusque went to the counter to order the coffee and cake. Diderot, Voltaire and the Montgofliers looked on from the other side of the room and whispered to themselves.

"According to our files," said Gentilhomme, "Leclair married for a second time, Louise Roussel, in 1730. She owned a lucrative engraving business and prepared all of Leclair's compositions for printing from Opus 2 onward. They were married for 28 years, apparently their happiness only falling apart over the last several years. It seems that Leclair struck out on his own to get rid of a nagging wife who was going through menopause, who no longer enjoyed intimacy, and who argued with him constantly about whose money was whose.

According to a neighbour, Leclair confided in him that he wished to be rid of the wife, so that he could live alone in an apartment or a little house, and finally have his own freedom. He said he wanted to have independence and cultivate female relationships on his own terms, even if it meant getting a mistress or a prostitute. The neighbour said Leclair wanted to spread his wings. He finally purchased a small house on his own, though it was from a seedy landlord, Monsieur Legras, who promised to repair things for a small fee each month if any work needed doing. Somehow things always came up, spring or winter repair, the leaky roof, drafty windows, and the uneven cobble stones in the walkway. There was always something! Which Leclair shied away from because he preferred that someone else's fingers got pinched. Leclair was no good as a handy man and liked to spend his time instead, reading comfortably by the fireplace, smoking his pipe, and of course, composing music at his desk or practicing the violin at all hours.

By the time they had drunk their second cup of coffee and disposed of their cake, the trio of officers concluded that the ex-wife was indeed a perfect candidate for the murder. She may not have had the strength, but possibly, one of her male co-workers could have been hired to kill Leclair with an engraver's tool from the shop, maybe a "bright-cut engraving tool" or a "knife graver" which could make deep cuts.

During the investigation of Leclair's whereabouts on the evening of his death, they found out that the man had been playing billiards at his favourite tavern with a friend who was also a musician. They had interviewed that friend first thing and found no reason for suspicion there. Just an amicable game of billiards which Leclair and the friend routinely played to wind down the day. The friend said that Leclair chose to sit for a while by the window and sit privately for a time sipping his wine and nibbling on cheese. Then he got up and left. The friend added one more item of note, Leclair's nephew was there in the tavern that night, sitting in the far corner seemingly entertained by the tavern's tipsy revelers. But then the nephew routinely did that and chose never to sit with his uncle, although he would occasionally play billiards and sit and gossip with other customers.

The police had something to go on by that time, in terms of background and persons of interest. Procope's coffeehouse actually made the investigation fun. The Lieutenant knew enough about managing people's productivity by including a few humane perks in the work. Now the next task was to actually interview the ex-wife. The Lieutenant suggested going over to her shop. That way, they could actually see all the instruments and engraving tools which were available to a potential murderer or murderess.

As the police sauntered out of the door at Procope's, carting away their files, the intelligentsia in the room whispered amorphous things about the departing presence of the police. The Lieutenant of Police, Antoine-Gabriel de Sartine, only smiled as he shut the door of the coffeehouse behind him.

Chapter 6

November 4, 1764

The three officers stood at the door under the sign of "Louise Roussel, Engraver" in the Rue Saint-Jacques. De Sartine turned to Gentilhomme and said, "Why don't you do the honours and knock?" A big iron door knocker faced them, shaped like a large treble clef. "Hmm," wondered Gentilhomme, "I wonder if it plays music when you knock?"

When Gentilhomme did as he was told, it was Louise Roussel herself who opened the door. She eyed the three men up and down and realized they were not there to bring her business. She was curt. "What do you want?" she asked. Lebrusque countered, "As the ex-wife of the recently deceased M. Leclair, we need to interview you, Madame. We are the police."

"Ah, the boys in blue!" she said.

The lady made them wait for a moment or two, just to show them she could. She was past working age, they judged, so she probably was not in a financial position to afford the luxury of retirement. Approximately, 65 years of age, judged the Lieutenant. She reminded him of an old crow, lean and thin, with a small beak extended from a wrinkled face. Maybe age had extended that beak somehow. "These must be the lean years," thought de Sartine. She finally let them in and guided them past her place of business, an assortment of engraving machines on the floor, and an array of cutting tools strung up on the walls. One large man was bent over scribing into a metal template. When he rose, he showed an evident limp.

"We also print musical scores," commented Mme Roussel as they went by her co-worker. She led them into her inner office and asked them to sit. The large man limped over carrying two chairs, one at a time, and then left.

"Now then," she said. "What can I do for you gentlemen in blue?"

Lebrusque got to the point. "Where were you on the night of October 22nd or the early morning of October 23rd?"

"I was sound asleep in my quarters upstairs," she said. "I find that arrangement economical, especially since my business has suffered a setback in recent years."

"Because your husband left you," asked Lebrusque tersely.

"Why yes," she confessed. "Because and ever since he left me."

"Why did he leave you?" asked Lebrusque.

"That dear Officer, is none of your business," she retorted.

Lieutenant de Sartine cut in. "Quite right Madam. For the moment, it is none of our business." He took over the questioning. "However, can you prove you were at home during the night of October 22nd and the early morning of October 23rd?"

"Only if sleeping with André is proof," she chuckled. "We are a couple. He likes older women. Just loves my blue eyes and my dimples, if you've noticed!" She called out, "André come in here, were we or were we not sleeping together last week on Monday, October 22nd and Tuesday, October 23rd?" He limped to the door and blushed. "Why, as a matter of fact, every day of the week!" he acknowledged with a broad smile. "There," said Madam, "my alibi!" And proudly she added, "One that is clearly 20 years younger than I."

De Sartine backed off, not wanting to get into the business of their bedroom which was of no concern to him. When Madam realized that the Lieutenant was backing off somewhat, she relaxed. Tears rose in her eyes. She took a breath and talked about her former husband. "I did love him you know." She reminisced, "Those were good years when we first started out."

She explained that a woman goes through changes, and when her menopause hit, she felt moody and argumentative. She also did not feel attractive and so was disinterested in her wifely duties to her husband in the bedroom. "That's when the marriage fell apart," she said, "we slept in separate bedrooms." Madame explained that her husband started going out at night to taverns. He preferred Le Coq d'Or, a higher-end establishment, not like La Dame Chantante, which served a lower class of people. They went through 7 years of uncertainty and insecurity like this until he got the notion to trundle off to Holland with his violin, to leave the country, and leave Louise and daughter Little Louise behind in France with the business while he cavorted around with lords and ladies at the court of the Princess of Orange at Leeuwarden.

He became a changed man, a different one who needed love and pity when I first met him, when his first wife took ill and died. Louise confessed that it was difficult to keep her business' finances solvent after he left because he'd visit Paris now and again and then be off back to Holland or heaven knows where. "After more years since he went to Holland, we finally divorced in 1758. He was a career husband married to his violin, and my little Louise needed a father who was never there." She added, "For old time's sake, however, he brought me his future compositions to help out with our business and our living.

"I kept my business going with other small commissions," she said, "but found it convenient to move in with a Monsieur Chavagnac on Rue du Four-Saint-Germain after our divorce. It was funny that a former patron, the Duke of Gramont, offered my husband the chance to move into his very own luxurious house, so that my husband could live with some dignity and respectability...and what did he do? He rejected the offer and decided to find his own place to live...in a dark and tiny, run-down hovel close to the Saint-Martin's canal. Can you imagine living by the canal on the dirty side of town, north of Le Marais? How completely insane is that, for a violinist to lower himself so? If he ever got into a brawl with a street thug, can you imagine the damage he could do to his delicate hands? My husband had some crazy notion about independence and living freely. He did not wish to rely on anybody's charity, and wanted to make it on his own, with his own talent, with confidence that his talent would pull him out of his financial problems."

Madame added as an after-thought that Leclair wanted to try out a libertine lifestyle; eat the poison fruit, so to speak, and enjoy other women before he died. "That's when he looked for prostitutes, and eventually a mistress," said Mme Roussel, with indignation. "I was no longer good enough for him."

"Madame" we know what happened to him during those unsettling years but what about you? Louise Roussel explained that her business almost went bankrupt, much of it as a result of her spiraling into years of menopause, but somehow, she kept her business afloat, and as her spirits lifted, she found that her business slowly got better. "I managed," she said, "with bumps and scrapes, as it were, but I survived."

She explained, "I know I've had financial difficulties; I've had them before. But Monsieur Legras has approached me recently to sell him the title of that little house back, north of "Le Marais". My husband still kept me in the will. There are some belongings which I wish to retrieve there, and I also wish to publish some more of my former husband's works which I have discovered in the house. I see light at the end of the tunnel."

Madame Roussel said she found her talk with the police most refreshing, and the Lieutenant especially kind. She never talked so much to police officers in her life. André had been listening at the door like a guardian angel. He got the hats and coats for the officers as they made their way to the door.

As the trio walked slowly past all the machines and the sharp tools, they judged that none of them seemed sturdy or wide enough to slice through a man's shoulder blade, even with the application of tremendous force. They were tools for artwork, scrolling and cutting fine lines in blocks of wood or metal for the printing process.

They each shook Madame's hand and walked out the door with the feeling that Madame Louise Roussel was indeed on the way up again and that indeed she had not perpetrated the crime, especially with a cripple at her side. It was clear that Madame Roussel's paramour, André, was not agile enough to run up behind Leclair and subdue him quickly with three forceful stab wounds in the back. The Lieutenant wished them well and hoped the business would soon improve.

As the door closed to Louise Roussel, Engraver, Gentilhomme nudged the Lieutenant's elbow, "Well, what do you think?" The Lieutenant said, "No murder weapon there. If we look at Leclair's body and match the wounds to a knife or sharp object, we will find that the width and depth of the wound most likely came from a broad bladed trade knife. Almost anyone in France could carry one of those for self-protection at night. It could even have been a Katar, a knife favoured in India. We do not have the resources to look into every possibility. I am at a loss. Who is next on the list?"

Gentilhomme flipped the pages of his notebook. "How about the mistress or a prostitute? But how do we find her?"

"Well, gentlemen, we won't do that just sitting here!" said the Lieutenant.

Chapter 7

October 22, 1764

Leclair did not like walking home alone from Le Coq d'Or at night. Most nights he did not even go to the tavern, but when he did, he hailed a carriage to take him to his little house in the northern part of "Le Marais". Carriages hovered around the taverns in Paris late at night, like vultures swooping in circles to scoop up clients, the prize being a fare and sometimes a tip of an "Écu au bandeau de Louis XV", which in silver currency was a handsome pay for one night's work for getting a drunken patron home without mishap.

There should have been a carriage visible down the street tonight, but none was this night. And yet, it had been a recorded fact, that there were more than 10,000 carriages for hire in Paris by 1750, the first taxicabs. But tonight? Nothing! "That's a nuisance," Leclair thought. He did not have the patience to wait, so he started walking instead.

Jean-Marie Leclair was ready to spend the "Écu" because he was not feeling that well. He confessed out loud, "By God, I must have had a good 5 glasses of wine in me this night!" He murmured, "Quaffing that much in one night will ruin my day tomorrow for practicing my fiddle. But I did it to myself. Nothing like an old fool."

He remembered a lot of sitting in the steamy tavern, looking at women, with an obvious intention of picking one up, a "femme fatale" which would give him one night of pleasure; it really didn't matter which one; he wasn't particular...but the opportunity came and went since he was too inebriated and too smelly to perform an "art d'amour" even if he were able to sweet-talk one of the women to come home with him. While he drank in the tavern, maybe his fifth glass of the night, he thought he spied his nephew, Guillaume-François Vial, sitting in the far corner, studying the scene with a shrewd eye. Maybe his nephew was there to beg for a letter of recommendation again to get into the King's Symphony. Leclair was tired of these repeated entreaties. They were becoming tiresome. Leclair turned his back away from his nephew, once he confirmed that the big man was actually there. He faced the window instead and concentrated on eating his slice of cheese and piece of bread in peace.

The talk in the tavern was tiresome too, more complaints about the increased taxes on wines, and the threat to use the hundreds of "guinguettes" or smaller taverns springing up around the outskirts of Paris like fireflies. Wine cost a third of the price there than inside of Paris. Perhaps Leclair would not have to run into his unwelcome nephew in one of those, whereas Le Coq d'Or was a more habitual haunt for both himself and Vial. Although wine, cheese and bread cost more, at least he could rub elbows with a more refined crowd.

"Still, I really do need to find a different watering hole," thought Leclair. He sneered in the direction of his nephew, thinking, "He is not that good a violinist anyway. He should be at home practicing his fiddle, even in these late hours, rather than wasting time here drinking wine in a noisy tavern." Leclair's eyebrows rose with the sudden realization that this advice could apply to himself as well.

Leclair had had enough. The women seemed to have their eyes set on younger men tonight. He finally decided to stagger towards the exit, stepping into the fresh air of the night. Leclair looked for a coach to hail, flashing a brand-new silver coin, an "Écu au bandeau de Louis XV".

There were no takers down the street, tantalized by the sight of the coin because they had all been taken by other drunken clients, so no coaches were in sight. Therefore, Leclair pocketed his coin and staggered slowly in the direction of his home in the Rue Careme-Prenant. "Oh well, I've got more money for wine next time around," he said to himself, and promptly vomited on the nearest lamppost on the street. The lamplighter for these streetlamps which were fired by oil was just finishing his rounds, not happy to see Leclair desecrating and then leaning against his precious lamppost. Who would clean up the mess? He ignored lighting this particular lamppost, and spit towards Leclair in disgust. "Merde!" he said.

Somehow by the grace of God, or the twinkling of the stars above, Leclair got home to his own walkway on the Rue Careme-Prenant. He was near his door when he suddenly felt a heavy blow to his back, a solid hit which was piercing and sharp. His right hand went up to reach back to his left shoulder, wondering if a rock had hit him. Some prank by a thug? As Leclair keeled over, a second blow smashed into his neck. He heard bone crack back there. "My god," he grunted, "I've been stabbed! However, will I practice tomorrow?" He felt a third blow in the back of his neck, and he keeled over, paralyzed. Finally, he fell face first onto the cobble stones. So close to the door of his own home. He dropped his book and also the musical manuscript which he clutched in his left hand. That manuscript sketched out the plan for a new Concerto, one in the key of E Minor, Opus 16. It would be quite lovely. It would never be heard.

After the first shock, Leclair realized he would never play violin again. "Oh, my beautiful Concerto," he lamented, "unfinished, and gone forever just like dust."

Someone grabbed him from behind and turned him over. "Who is it? What is happening?" He faced the night sky. He could see the distant stars twinkling high above, so delicately like the runs of an arpeggio on the keyboard. But the hateful eyes of his killer blocked the stars, and stared down on him, face to face. The eyes mocked him. He only saw those cold eyes, colder than the night sky. "Yes, I recognize those eyes," he thought, "I never thought you would do this to me." The lower half of the killer's face was covered by a black shawl, like a road agent's disguise. Leclair stared into those cold eyes and wanted to know, "Why?" But he already knew; it's just that he did not think he'd do it.

The voice said, "You've had your time, old man. Now you must get off the stage for young men like me to claim the fame. That is the order of things, and the way it has always been."

The culprit turned Leclair over again onto his stomach. He wiped his bloody hand on Leclair's overcoat, and as he did so, he felt the man's pocket watch. It was gold-plated. Why not take a memento? He snatched the watch and chain, and then got up with a nod of satisfaction. He took a deep breath and looked up at the twinkling stars himself. He raised a clenched fist to them, and said, "It is my turn to inherit them." He spit upon Leclair, as the man lay dying. He then sheathed the dagger and pulled Leclair into the vestibule, leaving the door wide open. He picked up the blood-stained book and the blood-spattered manuscript and threw them into the vestibule beside Leclair's dying body.

Leclair was not even sure if it had been the nephew, so drunk and shocked was he. And as he sank further into oblivion, the thought crossed his mind whether all of this was only a dream. After all, how could he be dying? His head swam, and he seemed to be floating far away up and up, beyond the last glimpse of the distant stars. But how could that be? He was lying face down in the vestibule, and that was absurd. "My Concerto!" he groaned, "unfinished. So much to do. This breaks my heart."

There lay at his side a book, Rameau's "Treatise on Harmony Reduced to Its Natural Principles" [1722]. The book had fallen open on a blood-soaked page which suggested ways in which to approach harmony and make it work. Beside Rameau's work lay a sheet of music with notes scribbled hastily on the page like chicken scratching, an incipient plan for a new Concerto. At the top of the spattered page was written, "Violin Concerto in E minor by Jean-Marie Leclair". One could hardly read the notes because of the blood stains. Which were the notes, and which were the blood stains? The killer hadn't bothered looking at these objects which he carelessly tossed into the vestibule beside Leclair's dying body.

The time was one minute to midnight. Jean-Marie Leclair would never hear the cathedral bell toll 12, and he would never live to see the new day and the new sunrise of October 23rd, 1764.

Chapter 8

Leclair the ballet dancer

"I feel really good. It's been a great rehearsal," said Jean-Marie Leclair wiping his brow. It was October 23rd, 1715. He was 18. His dance partner, the ballerina, Marie-Rose Casthanie, had worked up a sweat too. She wiped her hands on her colourful frock, and then dabbed her brow with a lace handkerchief patterned in floral designs. She was much older than Leclair but still quite slim and attractive.

She did not wear a tutu, of course, because that fashionable item did not make its appearance until 1832 when Marie Taglioni wore a gauzy white skirt cut to reveal her ankles at the Paris Opera. Baroque dancers back in 1715 made up for spectacle on stage by wearing colourful silk gowns, feathers and lace like the nobility; the men wearing three cornered hats, fancy coats with shiny fringes and pantaloons and stockings that covered the calf, all very colourful, gaudy and fluffy.

Ballet had taken France by storm ever since The Sun King, Louis XIV, had taken a small part in a ballet at the age of 14 where he represented the rising sun. It had become a tradition now to have fancy Balls at court featuring amateur and professional dancers. The Academic Royale de Danse was created in 1661 and now that Louis XIV had died at the age of 77 in 1715, the tradition continued more popular than ever in the courts of the nobility. The Lyons Opera was busy rehearsing for a Ball which was coming in several weeks hosted by the Duke and Duchess of Lyons before the Lenten season.

Marie-Rose looked admiringly at Jean-Marie attired in his cocked hat, red double-breasted coat, and maroon pantaloons. She imagined his body underneath, lithe and muscular like a whippet. "Your steps were impeccable today," she complimented him. "I do not know at which you excel the most, the dance or the violin?"

"Neither," he joked, "I love them both equally."

Marie-Rose was still stunning, especially to a 19-year-old. He felt special since an older woman found an interest in him. She stood there in front of him like a queen, regally outfitted in a fluffy blue silk dress, narrow at the waist with lovely folds billowing out beyond her dancer's narrow feet. Her coiffure puffed up above her head, held in place by a decorative hair comb shiny with pearls. He was only somewhat less resplendent wearing a white wig, ponytail at the back, his head topped with a red cocked hat, of the three-corner style. His coat was pink and his pantaloons maroon. They looked like human peacocks, proud, iridescent and precise. After all, they were dancers dressed to catch the eyes of an admiring audience in the 18th century.

Both of them had been retained as professional dancers at the Lyon Opera. They were rehearsing a Gavotte, as well as a Rigaudon, the Rigaudon requiring more energy because it was a sprightly dance, whereas the Gavotte required elegant precision. Occasionally, Jean-Marie doubled as a violinist for the Opera but was not paid double, because he was on contract. Four of his seven siblings, however, were retained as musicians by the Lyons Opera and thus added extra money to the family income.

The Duke and Duchess will be pleased," said Jean-Marie to his pretty dance partner. They were in love. He would be 19 next year, of marriageable age, already having had his parents' blessings. Perhaps, his parents had second thoughts though about his union, especially to an older woman, but then the father gave in, "Let him make his own mistakes." The mother secretly lamented, "I see black."

"Come let's go for another round," he said to Marie-Rose, "the Rigaudon still needs some more work."

Unfortunately, there is little history recorded on either Leclair or his bride-to-be at this point, not until they got married in February 1716, after which Jean-Marie started to make his mark as a dancer and musician of remarkable talent. Jean-Marie must surely have excelled in the art of dance because in 1722, a mere six years after the marriage, he was hired as first dancer at the Turin Opera. Yet, he remains an enigma because his marriage paper described him as a "braid maker", neither dancer, nor musician.

The next decade of their lives was rather unsettling because they did not stay in one place for long after their marriage. The stay in Turin, after 1722 was about a year. In 1723, the couple moved to Paris. Then within another three years, in 1726, the couple moved back to Turin. Then, in 1728, they bounced back to Paris. All of this must have been hard on the wife, especially an older wife. In 1728, Marie-Rose Casthanie died. There are only a few mentions of her in the history books. Two years after his first wife died, Jean-Marie married his second wife, Louise Roussel, in 1730, in Paris. She published and printed Jean-Marie's musical compositions.

It would be interesting to read between the lines and create some drama, a real story with dialogue between Marie-Rose Casthanie and Jean-Marie Leclair during those dozen years after their marriage with all the moving around they did. What might have been the real story if one applied an imagination beyond the bare facts. What did they feel? What did they think? Did they argue? What did they discuss over dinner? How often did they make love?

*****

Jean-Marie Leclair was born in Lyons, in East-Central France, May 10th, 1697. He was the eldest of eight children [another documentary says seven children]. The father, Antoine Leclair, was indeed listed as a "braid maker" by profession and apparently Jean-Marie did indeed learn this trade, among several others. The father was also described as a haberdasher by trade, who relaxed by playing the cello in his off hours. He and his children would presumably be called upon to play for various church functions and events in the city of Lyons, and occasionally be paid a bit of money.

Just to jump ahead somewhat, it is interesting that Lyons was the home of other famous people, like the Lumière brothers, Auguste and Louis, who invented the cinema or "cinematograph" in 1895. But jumping back to 1697, one might say the other invention which Lyons was famous for was producing Jean-Marie Leclair, a genius of the 18th century, who had a combined talent in dance and in the violin.

Nothing is mentioned of the Leclair matriarch. But the father, Antoine, with his non-descript wife, produced eight children, four of them musically gifted, and as young children, ready to provide the neighbourhood with the joyful noise of their instruments. The family lived crowded above their haberdashery shop. There were three girls and five boys.

The family included the oldest, Jean-Marie himself, born in 1697, then, Jeanne, b. 1699, Francoise 1701, Jean-Marie, "le cadet", [in English, the younger] 1703, Francois 1705, Antoniette 1708, Pierre 1709, and Jean-Benoit 1714. Four of these children became musicians, two of them making a minor mark on musical history. Pierre published a book of duets in the same year that his brother was murdered, 1764. Jean-Marie, the younger, also published works for two violins and a vocal work of no account.

It is interesting that Johann Sebastian Bach in Germany was fruitful in the number of his children, outdoing Antoine Leclair 8 to 20, with an amazing 11 Bachs becoming composers.

Maybe there is something to a crowded family developing music as part of their survival skills. There could be heated debate here about Nature versus Nurture, genes over upbringing. If one studied the lives of the Leclairs and the Bachs, a person of common sense would say that the outcomes in both sets of children was a happy mixture of genes, as well as upbringing. It's the academics who like to argue percentages, of which influence was the more dominant, which is not relevant to the weaving of this novel.

Compared to his father, Antoine, it is ironic though, that Jean-Marie Leclair only had one child, a daughter out of his two marriages, a daughter named Louise, who was not only named after her mother, but also became an engraver just like her mother, ignoring any musical gift from the father's side. The younger Louise later married a painter, Louis Quenet, thus putting a dead stop on Leclair's musical gene pool.

Chapter 9

Falling in Love

After kissing Marie-Rose Casthanie goodbye outside the door of the Lyons Opera, Jean-Marie Leclair walked home in a world of his own, light-headed and in love. His father, Antoine, had provided well for his family by 1715. Each of his children could follow their own dreams, provided they helped out with the family business. The haberdashery was thriving. "We Suit to Please," boasted the sign above the door. The haberdashery was known for its decent reputation of quality and honest service. The shop stocked a wide array of men's clothing, accessories and repair kits for coats and dresses. The shop sold needles and thread, sewing notions like buttons and ribbons, and advertised that pantaloons, frocks, coats and dresses could easily be altered, or made new, made to measure.

All the children had become adept in the trade. Jean-Marie even described himself as a "braid maker" and haberdasher, just like his father.

The mother was in demand as a seamstress and made all items of clothing for the Lyons Opera and the little theatre in the city, as well as for the ladies and gentlemen of the aristocracy who staged Balls and special events in the mansions of Lyons. In short, business was booming for the Leclairs, and they had the manpower to handle it with their eight children.

Yes, Jean-Marie was on top of the world. He had a loving family, huge talent, and a sweetheart [even though older] who adored him. He went home in a cloud.

"I'm home Papa, shouted Jean-Marie," as he sauntered in the door. "Good," said the father, "Go hold the cloth for your mother then."

Since Jean-Marie had been born in 1697, Papa Leclair had made substantial renovations to their domicile. The haberdashery where they worked and stored most of their wares was downstairs; the family lived and slept upstairs in a large space divided in three. The boys' bedroom, the parents' bedroom [which was also subdivided by a curtain for the three girls], and then the living quarters where they visited, practiced their instruments and ate their meals.

The downstairs was heated by a large fireplace, which always needed to be replenished with wood as the winter months approached. This need was already felt; now that October had descended upon this East-central part of France. It was a chillier October than they were used to. The family heated the upstairs with a modern German stove which took some maneuvering to get into the center of the living quarters upstairs because the stove had to be taken apart and then put back together again. Jean-Marie was useless at the task, but Papa Leclair figured it out. The family was snug and warm when they practiced their instruments there in the evening and visited before going to bed by 9:00 p.m. It was too bad that the Franklin Stove did not come on the market 25 years earlier, being invented much later by Benjamin Franklin about 1740. It was popularly called the "Pennsylvania fireplace", incorporating the basic principles of the heating stove. Papa Leclair could have afforded it back then, instead of purchasing the bigger and more cumbersome German stove. The main thing was, that the family did well financially, and they were comfortable in their living quarters, summer and winter.

John Hartig   Two Baroque Prodigies

Their daily routine was simple: early to bed, early to rise. They worked 12 hours each day. They retired at 9:00 p.m., got up at 5:00 a.m. Had tea, bread and a piece of cheese, practiced music for two hours until 7:00 p.m., had bread with an egg for breakfast, if they were lucky, and then opened the shop by 8:00 a.m. to start making clothes for the nobility. By 9:00 a.m. the shop was open for business. By 1:00 p.m., they closed up shop for two hours for a lunchbreak, until 3:00 p.m. They would be back at work until 6:00 p.m. and then have the shop cleaned and everything put away by 7:00 p.m. or so, when they had a late supper, called a "souper".

The only one exempted from this daily routine was Jean-Marie, the elder, because he had progressed so quickly at dance and at the violin that he was in demand for various pageants, plays and ballets put on by the Lyons Opera. The best part of this was that he was actually paid for something he loved doing.

Meanwhile, the rest of the family faced the same routine each day, but neither the parents nor the children minded because they got to play lots of music during various breaks, and in the evenings, they enjoyed each other's company, because unlike many working families, money was not an issue and they got along.

Now this did not mean that the Leclairs had an abundance of time on their hands where they played nothing but music. They did their chores like all the artisans and shops strung along the street adjacent to each other. Papa Leclair made sure that he had a broom and a bucket of water standing outside his shop, so one of the boys could sweep wayfaring urine and other unsightly stuff further down the street to the next shop. This was all a co-operative effort silently agreed upon by all the shops. However, if one shop happened to be recalcitrant and didn't do their bit, occasional inflammatory remarks could fly. It might take a while to get friendly again until that neighbour did his bit again in front street maintenance. No underground plumbing existed at the time to do a more efficient and civilized job of disposing human waste.

Papa Leclair's customers were ladies and gentlemen of the nobility, or the wardrobe mistress of the Lyons Opera, from whom they got lots of business, especially since their son, Jean-Marie was one of the key dancers and an orchestra member for the theatre. But there was only so much they could do about urine control, considering how everybody in the 18th century disposed of their waste.

The front of Leclair's "Mercerie" [haberdashery] could not avoid unwanted things floating down the street. Urine on cobble stones was a problem not only for his shop, but for all the shops down the street. Monsieur Frugé's "Boucherie" [meat], Madame Vincens "Boulangerie" [bakery] and Monsieur Franchessi's "Fromagerie" [cheese], even Monsieur Levesque's "Menuiserie" [carpentry], and Monsieur Bourassa's "Maroquinerie" [leather], all sported a broom and bucket outside their doors.

Urine could cause unsanitary damage to the bottoms of the flowing gowns of high-class ladies. Papa's broom and bucket just outside his shop were a sure sign that this was a store to come to because he was serious about keeping things clean for his clients.

At least, wealthy ladies had the means to have fringes and trim sewn into the lower edges of their dresses. These were washable fringes and needed to be replaceable because dresses which dragged along the cobble streets as ladies walked along, unfortunately soaked up the inevitable urine. It was a stinky time, the best of times and the worst of times. And dresses were brought into the

Leclair haberdashery on a continuous basis to be cleaned and to be fixed.

Wealthy ladies who entered the Leclair "Mercerie" also asked Madame to make dresses with fine silk, so finely woven that it kept the fleas out. Ladies of the nobility could easily afford most anything, and Mme. Leclair did not mind the extra work or the extra money for cleaning or repairing the filthy outfits which were brought into the shop. Often the ladies would walk out of the store with an unexpected purchase of a brand-new dress which was the latest rave. Because the Leclairs were middle-class, they could not afford to dress in high fashion themselves, but they could supply the materials for that, and so the Leclairs grew rich, if but slowly, on their own terms.

Chapter 10

Living in the 18th century
Sleeping arrangements in the Leclair household were simple. Boys on the one side upstairs, parents and the three girls on the other side, divided by a curtain. Little Jean-Benoit slept with the parents because he was only one.

The boys had two "closet-beds" on their side which were enclosed furniture units with a door. After a four-week trial period, it was decided that each of the older boys would sleep with a younger brother to keep them from being silly at night. Jean-Marie, the older, was 18, so he took Pierre who was only 6. Jean-Marie, the younger, was 12, so he took Francois who was 10. This arrangement kept a lid on the silliness at night. Because of the nature of boys, the two youngest ones poked each other if they slept together and made a big deal if somebody farted. It was understood that chatting quietly was tolerated before everyone settled down for the night, but not when silliness occurred. However, by the time the door to the closet-beds was closed, and sleep overcame them, the whole family was snug as a bug in a rug, even during the winter months. Their mattress was thick and fluffy, filled with hay, and so was their top blanket.

During the first four-week trial period for the sleeping arrangement of the younger boys, the complaints about farting was an irritating ritual every night, which kept everybody awake. Papa Leclair shouted a stern warning from his side of the room. "Stop it!" he yelled across the divide. If things did not settle down, the boys knew that a spanking was coming, which was a rare occurrence anyway, considering Papa Leclair's high tolerance level for nonsense in the household. If Papa ever brought out his belt, however, that was when tolerance ceased, and a capital offense had been committed. This hardly ever happened though, because just knowing that the belt was there, was enough to settle the boys down. Papa had only to say a word once and obedience followed like the sun breaking through the clouds. Papa and Maman decided to switch the boys around though after one month. The girls seemed to be more civilized at night, just naturally.

Occasionally, somebody had to use the chamber pot which was positioned just outside the closet-bed, located at its end. The chamber pot thankfully had a tight lid on it. Different children were assigned to empty the pot in the early morning for their week's "potty duty". The Leclairs were lucky enough to have made a deep enough runnel in their backyard for waste, at least away from the garden where they grew tomatoes and cucumbers every summer. On the parents' side, there was another set of closet-beds, one for the parents and one for the three girls. Little Jean-Benoit had the privilege of sleeping with the parents until he was three, at which time he would migrate to the boys' side. By that time, Jean-Marie the older should be married and out of the house.

The wood panels on these furniture sleeping units were painted with colourful designs, so as to blend in as actual furniture during the day. Most people in the 18th century slept in a half-upright position in these closets because lying down was associated with death. Because of their littler size, the smaller boys were allowed some leeway to sprawl out in all directions at night. If there was a leg or sharp elbow that poked the older brother, the offensive body part could always be shoved aside. So sleeping was not perfect, but manageable.

A baker's boy would walk up and down the street each day and shout out, "Fresh Bread, Baguettes, Croissants", which had to be bought each day, or else the family would be eating dried out crusts. Papa Leclair always had a can inside the door filled with loose change to pay the boy. Occasionally he would buy "eau de vie" which was brandy from another street vendor, "for his nightly medicine".

The water bearer was yet another a vendor whose job it was to carry a bucket of water up and down the street, out of which he would scoop a measure of water for a fee. Public fountains also required a fee, and often fights would break out there between water bearers and domestic servants who were told to fetch water by the nobility.

All in all, the Leclair family lived well. And now their 18-year-old son, planned to get married by the following year. "Ah," Papa Leclair thought, "1716 will be an expensive year." Maman thought, "I see black!"

Chapter 11

The poor and the rich
The family's basic diet was bread, meat and wine. Watered down wine, for the children. The big meal was afternoon lunch from 1:00 p.m. until 3:00 p.m. which involved "une entrée" of a mixed salad, soup, or some terrine or paté. "The main course was meat, if it was affordable that week, or fish, with potatoes, rice, pasta, vegetables and an assortment of cheeses, local of course. The next big meal was "le souper" which happened after 7:00 p.m., routinely the end of the day's work.

It was during those two big blocks of time in which home schooling took place in the Leclair household. Everybody took a quick nap at 1:00 p.m. Maman got up first and laid out the dishes and cut the bread, and prepared a plate of cheese, the salads and soups. Papa would corral the young ones, along with the older children and herd them toward the corner table for their day's memorization of languages and discussion of themes. The children asked questions like, "Were all Italians lazy? Were the English really rude and had no manners? Will anything good ever come out of Poland?" Papa would answer, "You must always keep an open mind. Do not dress everybody in the same cloth!" He would point out that the Vatican was built by the Italians. And as to the English being rude? "Why Handel chose to live there." As for Poland, "We must wait and see."

Papa Leclair loved his wine and made sure that the family had plenty of it. Every few years he would make enough to last another few years. The first time when he made wine was before a big holiday when he put a "Signe

Fermé" [i.e., Closed Sign] on the front window. He got baskets of grapes from the local farmer, a trade-off for Maman fixing the pants for the farmer and his children. Papa would begin the messy task of loading the grapes into the press and then cranking the wheel. A bucket would catch the juice. The whole haberdashery smelled rife for days, right up to the rafters, downstairs and upstairs included. Maman said, "I don't mind the taste of my wine, but to smell it all over our lodgings, with the children there, that's more than I can stand." So, in future Papa Leclair made a deal with the farmer to do the grape pressing out there on the farm. Papa and the farmer split the work and they also split the wine. Papa brought plenty of bottles home for the fruit cellar. He stored the wine bottles down there, in wine racks, and on shelves the carpenter had built. Papa also placed few staples of meat and cheese on those shelves. Bread was bought each day from the Boulangerie.

Papa asked Jean-Pierre, "le cadet" i.e., the younger, to go into the fruit cellar one day and bring up two bottles of wine. One was to go to the carpenter's shop down the street. Monsieur Levesque had agreed to build some shelves for the family to hold volumes of music. There would be a friendly exchange of a bottle for carpentry service rendered. The other bottle was to go to Madame Vincens at the bakery because she was ailing. Papa told his young son to tell her, "No charge." Bartering was a customary practice to avoid the exchange of money and to avoid taxes. Finding ways to avoid taxes in France became a national pastime.

People were usually generous with each other, bartering and sharing their skills, admittedly not just out of a good heart, but as a means to avoid taxes. Despite the growth of the middle-class, more and more poverty was noticeable, as were homeless people in 18th century France. They were called "les clochards" [the bums]. Paris seemed to be overrun, and Lyons was only a little better with rising poverty. All shops and houses had bars at the doors and shutters on the windows, which one can still see on houses to this very day in cities in France.

It would be wonderful to get a government grant to search tax records for the Leclair haberdashery through the 1740s to see how well the family was doing. But then those records stored at city hall were probably ribbed or burned up by the peasant mobs storming government offices during the French Revolution. Better yet, it would take a miracle in a time machine to track the prosperity of the Leclairs after Jean-Marie left home. Instead of making a living just out of the gowns and coats for Lords and Ladies of the Kingdom, did they diversify their sources of income to include military uniforms? After all, the thing which distinguished Napoleon's army from the Duke of Wellington's at Waterloo was the colour and cut of their uniform.

Likewise, one would wonder what really has changed in society, between those people in power and the poor. France's King Louis XVI was dethroned and decapitated. Emperor, Napoleon Bonaparte, took his place, in fact crowning himself...and the question remained, had anything really changed? At least, some professions had steady jobs, like metal workers for swords, guns and horseshoes, haberdasheries for uniforms and ladies' gowns and coffin makers, once those uniforms were shot to pieces.

So, Rich Man, Poor Man, Beggarman, Thief, the social order seemed to remain constant, moving along in any century, despite revolutions and the search for a utopia. King, Emperor, President or Dictator, what did it matter?

Top dogs were top, and bottom hounds always seemed to fight with each other to survive.

Haberdashers, like undertakers, were always employed. Somebody had to make those splendid uniforms with fancy buttons, epauletted jackets and hats with feathers, so one army could tell the difference from the other arm, so they'd know whom to kill. There is room for justified cynicism here about political movements and the masses through the French Revolution and beyond. One thing is clear, the Leclairs would have done very well indeed in peace or in war. They were blessed and lucky to make such a good living in the first half of the 18th century.

France got into a huge mess in the War of the Austrian Succession which lasted from 1741 to 1748, a 7-year war. It was an involvement where prized colonies were lost, and equipment, men, horses and uniforms cost lots of money in a foreign campaign. It did not help either that alliances kept changing during that time period. Louis XV and his 90-year-old adviser, Cardinal de Fleury, were too weak to argue against the vested interests of their courtiers. The national debt sky-rocketed to 2,200 <u>million</u> "livres" in 1763, just one year shy of Jean-Marie Leclair's ignominious murder. Jean-Marie of course didn't care about his country's woes by that time because he was dead!

The Royal Court was already squeezing the lower classes dry, hence the growing masses of poor people. How do you pay the debt? Who will pay for it? The King looked to the privileged classes to remedy the situation by taxing them more. But this was difficult to accomplish!
The privileged classes ran the "parlements" of the kingdom. They had paid for and owned their positions or inherited them for life and were considered irreplaceable, which of course, made the whole bureaucratic structure

corrupt. The privileged classes did not want to pay for the debts of a losing war.

It wasn't until 1771 when King Louis XV showed enough backbone under his Chancellor Maupeou to exile members of the corrupt "parlements" of Paris to the provinces and to replace them with salaried officials. The Abbé Terray began tax reform for the King and by 1774 the budget almost balanced. That's when King Louis XV died of smallpox, and a weak Louis XVI took over the throne of France. The new King, dominated by his courtiers, ran the country back into debt. Educated men did not remain silent, and openly criticized the government and the King.
Diderot and d'Alemberti continued to work on a collective project with 150 contributors to print their "Encyclopédie" which criticized "l'ancien régime" of corrupt customs and religion, arguing that society would be better off served by Reason and not a King.

In this context, Jean-Marie Leclair's family life and his teenage years, 1710-1716 [when he got married] were indeed blessed years. The family had it good. By the time of his murder, October 1764, Jean-Marie's country was so deep in the hole that anybody with a brain could see that a revolution was coming. One wonders how much a society can take before it explodes. It took 25years, however, after Jean-Marie Leclair's assassination, i.e., in 1789, for that social explosion to go off. The guillotine took the lives of King Louis XVI and Queen of France, Marie Antoinette, as well as many nobles, dukes and duchesses, who had ironically made the Leclair haberdashery rich.

Bastille Day, July 14th, became a national holiday for future generations. They thought they had gotten rid of the ills of society. The old order was swept away, the new order came in. The King was gone, Napoleon marched in, not as King but as Emperor, and it should be noted, an

Emperor who crowned himself. The question remained, did any of this solve anything?

The point, in retrospect, is that Jean-Marie Leclair and his family were lucky to have made their living in the first half of the 18th century. Yes, Jean-Marie Leclair could have picked a better part of Paris in 1758 to buy a house. He might not have been stabbed to death if he had lived in another part of town. He might have had a longer life, and more years of productivity as a composer before the French Revolution ever happened. But that speculation, like the question about whether The French Revolution could have been avoided at all, is a lovely discussion for academics over a cup of coffee. It could be an interesting question to pursue which a generous government grant could pay for, no?

Chapter 12

Musical Prodigy

There was something special about little Jean-Marie Leclair when he was three years old because his eyes lit up when Papa played his cello. The child swayed back and forth to the music and was annoyed when Papa stopped. From there on, Papa permitted the child to sit and play at his feet, both Leclairs, father and son, swaying in time to the music. That was the turn of the century, 1700.

When little Jean-Marie was a little older, about 5, his father stopped him and told him to put his baby violin down for a moment. Jean-Marie looked at his father as if he had done something wrong. "You did something clever," his Papa said. Jean-Marie did not know what, but he smiled bright eyed because little boys love getting praise, even if they do not know what for.

Mozart has gained an undeserved reputation as a child prodigy for composing the tune to "Twinkle, Twinkle Little Star" at the age of 5. The tune was actually a French melody, "Ah, vous dirai-je, Maman," published in 1761. The English lyrics came later in 1801, published by Jane Taylor. Mozart probably swayed to the music that his father, Leopold, played but "Twinkle Twinkle Little Star" is one credit for little Mozart at the age of 5, which is false. He did write 12 variations to the simple tune when he was 25 years old, just for fun. The point here is that prodigies, like Mozart and his predecessor, Leclair, show their gifts early. That is why they are prodigies. Leclair displayed that gift way back in 1707 when he was 10 years old and even earlier.

John Hartig   Two Baroque Prodigies

At the age of 10, Jean-Marie already knew what he wanted to be "when he grew up". His father felt that the age of 10 was a magical number for gifted children where some imprint or impression naturally came to them which would make music their destiny for the rest of their lives. Jean-Marie Leclair knew that the violin was part of his soul. Father and son, by 1707, played duets together, their most favourite pieces being the minuets, gavottes and gigues, composed by Jean-Baptiste Lully, which usually accompanied dances and ballets at the opera.

When Jean-Marie found out that his hero Lully was not only a violinist but also a dancer, Jean-Marie's said to himself, "I should be able to do that." Thus Jean-Marie began his dancing career at the Lyons Opera, at the age of 10, volunteering in bit parts at first and more involved things later. He got lessons from his father's friends at the Opera because there was always a demand for little boys in their theatrical productions of "opéras comiques" and even in Lully's "Tragédie en musique". By the time Jean-Marie was 15, he had acquired skills as a ballet dancer and had bettered himself as a virtuoso violinist. Whenever he would play a solo, Jean-Marie's eyes would glaze over and he would be transported into another world. The dance became his second love, but he could never make up his mind which discipline to follow to make his living. He was only sure that being an artist, in either dance or violin, was what he wanted to do "when he grew up".

When Jean-Marie was 16, Jean-Phillipe Rameau came to town, spending a couple of years there between 1713 and 1715. Rameau was 30 years old, and at the height of his powers. Lully had been dead already for 26 years, stomping his foot accidentally with his conductor's staff during a performance for the Sun King, Louis XIV. He smashed his big toe which got infected and eventually caught gangrene. He refused to have his leg amputated, and so, stubborn as he was, Jean-Baptiste Lully died, taking all his talent with him to the grave in 1687. Perhaps there is something to be said for being replaceable. There are and were clever people born all the time. After Lully, Jean-Phillipe Rameau was one of them, and at a later date, Wolfgang Amadeus Mozart was another.

When Rameau made Lyons his home back in 1713 or 1714, he worked for the Lyons Opera, at least until 1715, during which time he contributed a few "grands motets" to the Lyons Concert. He gave a little performance as well so he would astound people with his virtuosity. The 16-year-old Leclair was impressed by Rameau's flashy fingers on the strings and loved the show. He said to himself, "One day I will do that."

However, by sheer coincidence, Leclair and Rameau met earlier when Rameau first came to town in 1713. He swept into the foyer of the theatre with an air of importance, and upon spotting the young Leclair, Rameau asked, "Well, where is my dressing room?" Jean-Marie didn't know what to say, "Well, we don't have a dressing room as such. All we have is that back room there where everybody gets changed before we go on stage." Rameau patted the 16-year-old boy on the shoulder patronizingly, and commented, "This is a real hick-town, isn't it?" Jean-Marie was speechless, and finally replied, "I guess it is." He thought afterwards, "Paris must sure be some sophisticated city." Rameau was in Lyons long enough to actually see young Leclair dance in a ballet once, and also hear him play his violin briefly in a small orchestra. He said to himself, "That young man will go far someday."

Jean-Marie got married just three years after he met Rameau. He was 19 in February of 1716, and madly in love with Marie-Rose Casthanie, his usual dance partner in the

Lyons Opera. His parents did not like the fact that she was so much older than he. But what are you going to do with a willful teenager? He brought Marie-Rose flowers every week, and she enjoyed the attention. He asked Marie-Rose's mother if he might call upon her regularly on Sunday afternoons. The parents always stayed in the room with them, engaging in frivolous conversation, except several times when the couple was allowed to stroll around in the back garden during the summertime. This was all under the watchful eye of the parents who stood at the back window which overlooked the garden.

Marie-Rose was self-conscious about her age. "I'm so much older than you," she said, "will you still love me when I'm 64? I will grow old and ugly before you do." He protested, "You will never grow old and ugly in my eyes." As a dancer, she had maintained her figure and taken care of her looks. Jean-Marie did not look or think beyond that. What he said as a teenager in love, said something good about his good intentions. But good intentions and promises are one thing when you are young, and another thing in real life, when that determination is tested as the years go by. One good thing is that the marriage lasted 12 years, until Marie-Rose died in 1728, and that for a young Leclair was, one would suppose, a respectable fact.

On the day of the ceremony on a cold, cold February day in 1716, the couple got out of their carriage in front of Saint Jean Cathedral in the old part of town. The gathering of special friends and relatives was small. They decided to go cheap with a small crowd, though they splurged on being driven to the church in a carriage. The reception was held in Marie-Rose's large home which was more spacious than the inside of the Leclair haberdashery blocked by aisles of clothing and sewing articles.

Marie-Rose's parents provided a substantial dowry, and the Leclairs matched that sum. Jean-Marie and Marie-Rose put the money into a down payment on a small house in the old part of town. Since the house was a fixer upper, they hired a handy man to repair the roof and build some shelves. Jean-Marie knew about the violin, dance and haberdashery, but he knew nothing about carpentry and using his hands on crude work. He knew enough to protect his fingers for violin playing, which afforded him enough money at the Opera to pay somebody else to do the manual labour. It was amusing that in his marriage certificate, instead of violinist, ballet dancer or lace maker, he put down "braid maker", same profession as his father.

The couple lived happily in their little home for 6 years and often visited both sides of the family alternating them for Sunday meals and chatting with coffee and cakes in the afternoons. No children ensued. Both mothers-in-law were disappointed. No grandchildren! The couple were a career couple instead. They could have invented the word, "workaholic".

By 1722, Leclair got tired of the same old routine in Lyons. They had been married 6 years, and nothing was happening in his life. He was 25 and wanted to spread his wings, to grow and get famous and possibly rich.

"But I don't want to move," argued Marie-Rose.

"Don't you see," said he, "what a wonderful opportunity it is to move to Turin? They've offered me a job as principal dancer at the Turin Opera." This would mean not only moving out of the city but also into another country. Turin was the cultural center of the Piedmont area of northern Italy. At least, they both knew the language, since educated people and the nobility in those days knew several languages.

She countered, "I like our happy home here. We've made it a comfortable place to come home to at night, even though it is quite small and modest. But it's ours and we can afford it."

Well, Leclair insisted. He wasn't getting any younger at 25. He accepted the job as "first dancer" at the Turin Opera. It was an offer he could not refuse. Besides she also had a job as a support dancer with the troupe.

The rest if the family stayed in Lyons and continued their lives as usual. Jean-Marie Leclair, the younger, was now 19, the same age as his older brother had been when he got married. At the moment, he had no thoughts about marriage himself, but he knew he was happy to stay in Lyons where he could build a good reputation for himself as a violinist and composer in his own right. Although he did admit to himself that he was riding somewhat on his older brother's coattails.

Meanwhile, the older brother reasoned with his wife, "Things will turn out alright, you'll see." They sold their sweet little house, having made it attractive after several renovations, which became a real selling point. They got a good price for their investment and arranged for the big moving day. At least, part of the Turin contract provided that things would be packed up for them and moved. They would not have to lift a finger.

"It's nice to be wanted," said Leclair. So, a new era opened up for them, even though that era involved anxiety, especially for Marie-Rose, being older, as to what the future would hold. "It's an adventure," said Jean-Marie. His crystal ball only saw opportunity, and not displacement every few years from town to town. Marie-Rose was a lot like Jean-Marie's mother who saw black. But then Jean-Marie wondered if all women were like that?

John Hartig   Two Baroque Prodigies

The bare listings of dates and events up to this period in 1722 for the Leclairs are sparse, but the chance for imagination around these facts abounds. One can easily fill in the cracks by creating details like a baby Jean-Leclair swaying in time to the music at his father's feet, learning ballet at the age of 10, the courting ritual to win his wife, the marriage ceremony and buying a little house, and even the pretended meeting between Rameau and Leclair in 1713. All of these "happenings" are fiction, and enjoyable literary inventions. Otherwise, we would have nothing to add to an 18th century murder mystery. It is unfortunate that details are so sparsely recorded in this man's life and that the murderer was never caught. Perhaps the murderer created his own hell on earth through a guilty conscience for the rest of his life?

Chapter 13

The young Leclair

Recorded detail about Jean-Marie's life becomes more solid after 1722, after the move from Lyons, once he spread his wings into the new cities in France and Italy where he would become famous. It was only after the age of 25 that he made his mark as a virtuoso violinist and composer. He decided to take his teacher Somi's advice to concentrate on his violin playing and composing and not his dancing.

From then on there is more flesh in recorded history, but even in the last half of his life, there is still plenty of room for conjecture and a chance to build a fictional world around the hidden facets of the man's life and to invent a good 18th century murder mystery.

"And we didn't have to lift a finger," said Leclair staring up at the apartment which the board of the Turin Opera had provided for them. Mind you, it was not located on the posh side of town, but nevertheless, it was their new home.

"I miss our little house in Lyons, "said the wife. "Home is what you make it," replied Jean-Marie cleverly. "Home is where the heart is," he added glibly, "and that is with you, my dear." The wife felt like she was being patronized. Jean-Marie already felt, at the age of 25, that 6 years of marriage were dragging him down. Just that past February, they celebrated their 6th wedding anniversary. Time seemed to fly by so quickly. February! Why did they ever pick February to get married in?

After 6 years, he felt the stirrings of a secret unease. Deep down, he wasn't as fond of his wife as he used to be, though he still remained faithful. Marie-Rose wasn't stupid; she picked up on his cooling towards her. At a private moment, she faced him head-on and said, "Jean-Marie I know things have gotten difficult between us lately. I know we can't have children. But whatever you do, please don't hurt me." He didn't say anything.

Even though his main occupation was ballet at this time, he felt less passionate about the art than in previous years. The more he thought about his violin, the less he thought about his ballet dancing. The more he thought about his violin, the more he yearned to be a published composer.

He felt like he was the featured headliner for the Tetra Regio of Turin under false pretenses, and yet, he enjoyed the big title, "first dancer and master of the ballet".

He did not want to upset his wife, so he said little about his desire to publish his music. At midnight, he worked on his Opus 1 in the little back room by candlelight. His Opus 1 was a collection of a few sonatas which danced around in his head. But the publication of these sonatas would have to wait and remain an unrealized dream on the sidelines. For now, the ballet gave them their bread and butter, and satisfied his wife. She was also hired by the Turin Opera as part of the agreement, which brought in extra money. The wife followed along in Jean-Marie's shadow, quiet, submissive, and asking few questions. He seemed so forceful about his dreams and what he wanted to do. She was simply overcome by his youthful exuberance and his energy. Marie-Rose could live quite contentedly with how they made their living at the moment.

It was after a performance at the Turin Opera, that Jean-Marie received a note from a Monsieur Antoine Bonnier to come to his private box. M. Bonnier was a wealthy financier, holding the office of Treasurer-General of the Etats de Languedoc in southern France. M. Bonnier had connections in Paris, and with the provision that Jean-Marie take the financier's son, Joseph, under wing as a violin pupil, the father could make things happen for Jean-Marie in Paris. Jean-Marie's infatuation with Turin didn't last long, barely a year, when the Leclairs packed up and found themselves moving yet again to Paris, the City of Light, in 1723. There, Jean-Marie Leclair finally realized his dream for being published. He dedicated his Opus 1, his First Book of Sonatas for Violin and Basso Continuo, to Monsieur Antoine Bonnier, who made good on his promise to connect Leclair with the right people.

There seems to be some discrepancy among sources about the years when the Leclairs bounced back and forth between Paris and Turin, but we will take the simplest one. Suffice it to say, that the infatuation with either city didn't last long, and within a few years, in 1726, Jean-Marie got up enough gumption to say to his wife, "My dear, we need to talk. The Turin Opera wants me back as 'premier danseur'. They've renegotiated my contract as master of the ballet for the theatre. I'm serious about taking the position. Besides you will get your old job back as an extra with the troupe." His wife said, "We could have saved ourselves a move by simply staying in Turin all along." Jean-Marie did not say anything to that.

Once back in Turin, they settled into a different apartment, within walking distance of the theatre. At last, it seemed like they had a life of calmness and composure. Leclair's spirit felt more complete these days, because now he was published.

He was so satisfied with himself knowing that his Op. 1 sonatas were in print. Leclair also composed some ballets which were used as postludes to two operas at Turin's

"Teatro Regio Ducale" in 1727. Ironically and unfortunately these scores have been lost. So, remaining in print and preservation of his publications was no guarantee to posterity. Perhaps a note about the notion of immortality.

Although he was not in Paris, the City of Light, he met some grand people in northern Italy. One of them was Johann Joachim Quantz, the great German flutist and Baroque composer who was in Turin doing a grand tour of Europe to promote the flute. Quantz was born in 1697, the same year as Jean-Marie Leclair. They had lots in common. Quantz had met Scarlatti in Naples and Handel in London.

After Quantz rubbed elbows with Leclair in Turin in 1726, he moved on later to impress the Queen of Prussia and then the Crown Prince, Frederick II, who decided to take up the flute. Quantz told the writer, Friedrich Nicolai, that he had to hide in a closet one time, when he was about to give Frederick a lesson, when the domineering father exploded into the room in an outrage because he disapproved of his son "tooling around on the flute."

"Complete waste of time," he shouted red-faced, "that infernal flute...and that Quantz!" Well, perhaps the words weren't exact, but the Crown Prince's father must have shouted something equivalent in German. This did not deter the Crown Prince, Frederick II, though, because he actually became quite a good flute player.

1726 also gave Jean-Marie the chance to improve his skills on his own instrument, the violin, while he earned his pay as a ballet dancer. At the grand old age of 29, Jean-Marie Leclair began taking violin lessons from Giovanni Battista Somis. Somis had been a pupil of the great virtuoso and Italian composer, Arcangelo Corelli. Somis was impressed with Leclair's musical talent. It should be noted that Somis also took on another violin student by the name of Jean-Pierre Guignon, who also figured in Leclair's life at a later stage in Paris.

While in Turin, Leclair showed his talents beyond merely dance and violin by dabbling in choreography for the opera, "Didone". "Didone" was based on the tragic love-story between Aeneas, hero of Troy, and Dido, Queen of Carthage. Leclair also squeezed in time for composition, for example, three intermezzi for "Semiramide", an opera by Giuseppe Maria Orlandini.

It was Somis who said to Leclair that he would do better to concentrate on the violin, instead of wasting valuable time dancing. One can imagine Somis putting his hand on Leclair's shoulder after a good violin lesson, "The violin will get you further and a career in it will last longer than in dance." There seems to be some discrepancy here whether it was 1727 or 1728 [or both] during which time Leclair headed for greener pastures in Paris. But it is clear that he did follow Somis' advice to make the violin his mainstay for fame and fortune. Spreading his renown meant moving between Turin and Paris. This must have been difficult for his wife who dutifully followed.

Chapter 14

Getting Known

Once ensconced in Paris, in 1728, though not specifically clear exactly when, we are informed that "soon" he travelled to London and to Kassel.

In Kassel, Jean-Marie Leclair met Pietro Locatelli where the two of them staged a battle of the violins, French and Italian styles of playing, which people loved. Leclair's playing was angelic, marked by a beautiful tone, with rhythmic freedom. By contrast, Locatelli's playing was aggressive with a scratchy edge where he purposefully played "like the devil", perhaps a harbinger of the style adopted years later by Paganini. This was all showmanship and deliberately designed to entertain the journalists who wrote sparkling reviews for their papers.

During all this time, while Jean-Marie Leclair travelled and showed off, one wonders where Marie-Rose, his wife, was and what her thoughts were about the rising fame of her husband, and about whether he remained faithful to her. We do know that, coming back to Paris in 1728, Leclair published his Opus 2, which was a Second Book of Sonatas for Violin and possibly Traverse Flute. Now, he was truly published and famous!

This time, Leclair dedicated his music to Bonnier's son, Joseph, who inherited his father's money and hotel after the older Bonnier died. Joseph Bonnier became Leclair's new patron. Apparently, as part of the bargain, the young Bonnier wanted to continue in free violin lessons from Leclair, in return for which Leclair and his wife would get free lodgings at the Bonnier hotel. This seemed like an equitable arrangement, a perfect example of what goes around, comes around.

When the Leclairs were shown their luxuriant rooms in the hotel, they were awed by the opulence in each and every room, the furniture, the chandelier in the living room, the breakfast nook with large windows, the water closet even. M. Bonnier smiled and said, "You must be pleased?" Jean-Marie beamed, "We are, we are, and ever so fortunate!" "Well," said Bonnier, "my father was fortunate when he first started out as a financier, and as he always told me, by boy, it helps to have money. Remember money makes money." "Hmm," said Jean-Marie, "remind me to retain you as my financier." They both laughed.

The friendship with Monsieur Joseph Bonnier de la Mosson paid off in dividends, not only in lodgings, but also in networking with the big who's who. The friendship also gave Leclair a steady income in a pension from the young Bonnier's gratitude for teaching him the violin.

In the meantime, Leclair had other income. He performed twelve times as a virtuoso violinist for the "Concert Spirituel" which launched a new public concert series. His performances drew enthusiastic applause, and he was asked back repeatedly to perform his own sonatas and concertos. The young Bonnier also opened doors for Jean-Marie's wife, so that she could get a job as a dancing coach in Paris teaching well-to-do young ladies in the art of becoming ballerinas. Mme Leclair was in her 40s by this time, less capable of springing about on the dance floor. Instead, she verbalized and pointed out to young ladies what needed to be done in a dance. The young ladies adored her and listened to the experienced teacher.

Not much is known about why or how the health of his wife degenerated, nor what the private situation of their relationship was. The bare fact we know is that the Leclairs moved back to Paris in 1728.

Jean-Marie might have already met Louise Roussel, by that time, and with his first wife, Marie-Rose, being older, less healthy and less capable, he might have sparked some sexual interest in Louise Roussel. Perhaps, the fact that Marie-Rose could not have any children also gave him "leave", as it were, to let his eyes wander to the greener grass on the other side. Someone suggested that Marie-Rose did indeed get pregnant and might have died because of a difficult childbirth. It might simply have been just getting sick because she was older, and not having health care and poor meds, she went downhill and finally passed away. After all, this was the 18th century!

Leclair was only 31 at the time and had enough vim and vigour in him to let his eyes wander across the fence, sick wife or no sick wife. Whether he kept what he should have kept inside his pants is also a guess, as to how faithful the man was to his older wife, and to his marriage of 12 years.

But we cannot accuse him of being a philanderer at this time, because there are no records saying that he was one. Maybe a good case for philandering could be applied to his Parisian years after 1728, after Marie-Rose died. He was more famous then, more published, and moved around a lot from town to town. He also hobnobbed with the rich and famous, and they of course, afforded a different lifestyle and a set of mores beyond what the working middle class, like his parents, could afford. Money and success, and becoming a new bachelor, can change a person. Anyway, the seeds for a "transition" were already sown when Jean-Marie Leclair met Louise Roussel in her engraver's shop.

Louise Roussel was three years younger than Jean-Marie. In 1728, that age difference seemed to be a better match than with his own wife, Marie-Rose. Louise was 28 and Jean-Marie was 31. Marie-Rose's age was never specified in the history books, except that she was "much older" than him. Perhaps that age difference was 14 or 15 years, which would place her around 45? People in the 18th century seemed to age faster and die younger than what we are used to with our modern medicine and health care. It is also dubious that Marie-Rose would be pregnant at that age in those days, which would remove the argument that she might have died in childbirth.

Those things being said, Jean-Marie was attracted to a younger woman in 1728, one who looked fresh as a daisy. Ironically, by 1764 when Louise Roussel was 64 and when the police interviewed her as a possible suspect in her husband's murder, she had aged substantially and looked more like an old crow. But back in 1728, when Jean-Marie first walked into Louise Roussel's shop to ask about publishing his Opus 2 sonatas, he was smitten with a pretty face which far surpassed that of his wife. Louise Roussel on her part was not necessarily smitten by Jean-Marie's looks, even though he did look pleasant enough. She was more impressed by his obvious multi-faceted talents.

"Oh, a violinist...and a composer?" she asked.

"Well, yes, I'm guilty on both accounts, and maybe a third...I'm also a ballet dancer."

"My, my," she said coyly, "we don't get very many of those walking through the door. Let's see what we can do about getting your grand Opus into print. Number 2, you said?"

Since there are no records of Jean-Marie Leclair being a philanderer during his first marriage, we can say that he was faithful to his older wife. Though it seemed to be an accepted fact that men with status and money often had mistresses. But let's make Jean-Marie Leclair a somewhat nice guy. He was too busy with his work and composing to be distracted by dalliances.

Maybe his original family background gave him firm values from his Maman and Papa, and family life with his brothers and sisters. When Jean-Marie Leclair, at the impressionable age of 19, proposed to Marie-Rose, he was serious about his wedding vows. So, years later when his older wife started ailing after a few months in Paris, it seemed somehow like an extra betrayal, not to stay by her side. He couldn't live with himself if he were unfaithful at that time. Striking up an affair with Louise Roussel at this point, despite the intense attraction he felt for the woman, would be like stabbing Marie-Rose in the back. No, he could not, would not do it.

It is not certain if the first marriage had been generally a happy, though one likes to think so, because there are no records of friction or arguments between them. If one were to interpolate, one could argue that Marie-Rose might have been upset with her husband for being "a rolling stone" and moving from town to town every few years.

The wife might also have had her maternal instinct kick in, when she was still healthy, wanting something more in her life because she was childless. Not having children of her own and being an older woman, she might have asked her husband about adoption. She might have pointed out that Vivaldi might have been more prolific as a composer merely because he devoted his life to teaching orphans, as a service to God, in an all-female orphanage.

"Imagine what joy adopting an orphan or two could bring to our lives," she might have argued, "while we are doing the good work of Our Lord!" But these are speculations about their private lives and their feelings, something we know nothing about. Sadly, the only thing that is for sure, is that the couple had no children. The marriage could have been a happy one. It might have been a sad one. Who knows? Who knows if Leclair's mother's prediction, "I see black," ever came true about the marriage of that couple?

Thus, at the age of 31, we have the first part of Jean-Marie's life ending, wifeless and childless. A clean slate seemed to stretch ahead for the young violinist and composer when he lived in Paris in 1728. At least he played regularly at the "Concert Spirituel". It is a shame that there are so few records up to 1728 during the first 31 years of Jean-Marie Leclair's life. But at least, by this time, he was a published composer!

Chapter 15

Jean-Marie was required to visit Louise Roussel's engraving shop several times a week over the next two months. The shop was in the rue Saint-Jacques. He got there either by carriage or on a good day by walking with his walking stick as a sign of distinction. The visits were not just to finalize things about his Opus 2, but also to talk about other concertos and trios he had in mind for Louise's publishing house. Therefore, Jean-Marie had a legitimate excuse to get out of the apartment and go down to the shop and "confer with the engraver".

An acquaintance who had his artwork printed by Louise told Jean-Marie that, informally among friends, she was called "le petit moineau", The Little Sparrow.

"Why?" asked Jean-Marie.

"Her movements are so quick and precise, the way she gets things done, it is astonishing," replied the acquaintance. "Besides, everyone notices her pointy little nose which reminds one of a little bird." Jean-Marie made an internal decision never to call her Little Sparrow, certainly not to her face.

It seemed that affectionate friends had given her that moniker years ago, and she accepted it graciously as a compliment to her energy. Not that she couldn't be adorable like a little bird, but those who knew her in business, knew she could be a bird of prey. Keen eye for profit and the deal; she knew how to talk to people and turn a profit. She was also good at the physical work of her engraving trade. Engraving was a skill highly prized by women in the 18th century. Her father, Claude, would have been proud to see his daughter make the business work at a time when women were supposed to be kept home making babies.

Louise noticed from the beginning that the dedication in the masthead to Opus 2 was to Monsieur Joseph Bonnier. "Oh, the financier?" asked Louise. "Why, yes!" said Jean-Marie. "A friend of mine, a violin pupil and my patron." This opened up a whole line of discussion about whom in Paris they knew who was important. Louise brushed her hand over the manuscript and made a quick sketch for an idea of a masthead. She blushed as a thought popped into her mind. "I wouldn't mind sketching out your masthead," she thought, "and I don't mean this." Jean-Marie noticed, "Why, you're blushing!" She shrugged," Oh, I always get worked up about work. Leave the masthead, I mean your manuscript, here with me, and we will figure something out by Friday."

Jean-Marie was entranced by the look of her pretty face. She had light blond hair, braided in a long ponytail at the back, light blue eyes and deep dimples in her cheeks, which appeared like magic whenever she smiled. Jean-Marie found those dimples erotic. Perhaps the only fault he might find with her face was that her nose was pointy, like a little beak, but somehow that could be ignored because of her smooth skin, her full figure, and those dimples which could drive a man crazy.

"Oh, oh," he admitted to himself, when Louise Roussel first approached the counter and his eyes lit upon her smooth face and blue eyes, "here comes trouble."

He and Marie-Rose had lived in a protective bubble all these years. Nothing came from the outside to disturb their busy little world up until now. He had never experienced anything like this instant spark at the counter of the engraver's shop which brought temptation into his life like never before. He had always been able to put up blocks and concentrate on his violin playing and his compositions. But now there was something else. Perhaps it came with success and with the environment around rich people. Up until now, Marie-Rose and he had lived in a little world of their own, and had been reasonably content focusing on their work, i.e., mainly on his work.

His attraction for another woman was only afforded to a man who was physically healthy and had nothing wrong with him. In that respect, he could not identify with the other side, i.e. with his older wife's problems, who was suffering from ill health. Perhaps it was all the moving; perhaps it was simply that she was, after all, 15 years older than her husband. So, while she pulled in her horns like a snail, he was bushy and spry like a fox looking for mice. Not that he did anything about it at the moment, because after all, he had a conscience, a responsibility and work to take distractions away. But on occasion, something in the recess of his mind when he put his violin down to rest, something yearned. Health secretly seeks out its own pleasures, and Jean-Marie entertained those thoughts with a belief that it was natural in the order of things, and that, if something happened, then he could not help it.

He tipped his hat to Louise's dimples and smiled when he turned to leave the shop. The bell jingled when he opened the door and left.

The carriage still waited for him on the street. On his way back to the apartment, he did not realize how difficult the next few months would be with his wife, whether he had the loyalty and the stamina to stand by her.

He barely stepped in the door at the apartment, when Marie-Rose complained, "We should have stayed in Turin. It's been hard on me." She took a breath and looked at him sternly, "I've had more hot flashes lately, and the gout has broken out again on my toes. A dancer with gout is finished. I am grateful for the coaching job at the girls' school of dance, but even that is getting too much for me. I'm sorry we ever left Turin and moved to Paris."

He said in frustration, "But Paris is where I need to be to be published and to be noticed."

She said, "I thought you cared about my needs too? Didn't we speak endearments to each other when we were younger, and you said, you promised, that you'd love me even when I'm 64?"

Again, he looked at the ceiling and said nothing in response. He wished he did not feel trapped. That he was not here. Not with her. He was only 31 years old!

Jean-Marie wanted to run out into the street and yell. But no, he stayed in the apartment to listen to his wife run on about this and that and the other thing. How did they ever get this way?

Jean-Marie was convinced that Paris was where anybody who was anybody had to be to make his mark. Paris was where you get published so people would notice. Like usual, Jean-Marie listened to his wife droning on, adding to her list of ailments and dissatisfaction for just being in Paris. Why did they ever leave Turin or Lyons for that matter? Jean-Marie was not a happy man, and Marie-Rose had been noticeably looking sicker and sicker over the past two months. The City of Light looked less and less bright.

He looked forward to next Friday when he could confer with his engraver and get out of the apartment. Something positive to talk about, and some positive person to be with.

The doorbell jingled as he walked in. "Come to the back," invited Louise, "we can look at the proofs." They looked fine, the masthead looked fine, the dedication to Monsieur Joseph Bonnier was large enough, and his own name, stood out in an appropriate font, Jean-Marie Leclair, Opus 2, composer, 1728. He apologized to Louise if he did not seem as enthusiastic about the project as last week. He confided that his wife had been going through "the change" lately, hot flashes, and suffering from depression since her gout prevented her from dancing. "I do sympathize," he said to Louise, "how you can't be happy when you no longer do what makes you happy!" He needed a confidante so desperately...which meant not his wife, which over the next few weeks became Louise Roussel, more and more.

"Oh, you poor darling," said Louise. "Is there something I can do?" She patted his hand, stroking it lightly, and locked eyes with him. Her smile broke forth with those attractive dimples. "No," he said, "the words of a friend will be enough, at least for now. I know there have been feelings between us, but I have a duty to my wife...you understand?" "Yes," replied Louise, "let us be friends...for now. It would not be good to bring a guilty conscience into an affair with me."

That is how things fared for a few months until Easter approached. By that time, Jean-Marie Leclair got published again. His Opus 2 took Paris by storm and the King's court eventually took notice of the new talent in town.

The meetings on Fridays came and went quickly. Jean-Marie had been practicing all morning in March. By noon, Marie-Rose told him she needed a break from his playing. He said he would go out to check on the progress at the engraver's on the layout of some more pages. They ate in silence, and he walked out the door to hail a carriage. When he got to the shop, he was glad to see Louise. The day had been overcast and it looked like it would rain later on during the day. "Rainy days always get me down," he thought. It rained a lot in Paris. During March, with the

John Hartig   Two Baroque Prodigies

onset of spring and Easter weekend, clouds clung to the Paris skies and the city seemed in store for rain and even more rain, that year in 1728.

Chapter 16

Settled in Paris

The move to Paris should have been one of joy and renewal for the Leclairs, a hopeful restart for success. He was engaged at the "Concert Spirituel", one of the first public concert series, in the City of Light. His acclaim as an exceptional violinist was spreading throughout the city. The precision and refinement of his playing won him an enthusiastic following. He got what he wanted. Yet, his wife of 12 years was sick, too sick to share his joy, too sick to dance, and too sick to be a wife.

"You will leave me?" she asked.

"No, my dear, that is your sickness talking. I will not leave you."

M. Bonnier had seen to the medical expenses for Jean-Marie's wife. He paid for the doctor and for the medications. Leclair was ever so grateful to his benefactor. When Jean-Marie came home, either from his performance at the "Concert Spirituel" or from a practice there, he made his wife drink chamomile tea. Then he would rub eucalyptus oil on her back and on her chest. He was careful not to get any of the ointment on her nipples because that would sting.

"Do you remember when," he'd say, "when we did this for pleasure? We talked about love then and not plumbing." He chuckled; she didn't think it was funny. Sometimes he put some of the pungent oil into boiling water and made her hover over the basin with a towel to clear her breathing. But the situation was more serious, he realized, that it was not a mere flu or cold, or in her breathing. Once her ritual with the towel over the basin was done, he would carefully open the door and carefully toss the water out the door onto the street. This was a nightly ritual in the month of March. With his ministrations to her, he would always say, "Do you remember when..." Marie-Rose was not getting any better. The doctor prescribed making tea at night with Root of Valerian, adding a spoonful of honey with it, to help her sleep.

Jean-Marie was subdued and noticeably taciturn during his review of the new engravings in the print shop. He shied away from eye contact with Louise. She sensed his mood and accommodated him by going through the review that Friday in professional silence. He gave his nod of approval and said to her, "My wife is very ill. I will see you next Friday." The doorbell jingled as he went out.

During Holy Week, he had to play at the "Concert Spirituel" several times. It gave him some reprieve from the apartment. He fed his wife broth. They ate quietly, and then she said, "You will probably find another. I am sorry that I cannot share your success or your future with you." She hesitated, "But in the meantime, I want you to be faithful. If you do not come home tonight, things will never be the same again between us. Please, do not hurt me." Jean-Marie nodded. He guided her to bed. She rested her head on his shoulder. Her thoughts before she dropped off to sleep were, "When your own health and talent are taken away little by little, you get so dependent on others, too dependent. I do not know what I would do if he did not come home back to the apartment?"

Once she fell asleep, he kissed her on the forehead lightly. She had a fever, but he needed to escape the enclosure of the apartment. He put on his cape and hat, and quietly closed the apartment door. It began drizzling outside. He walked resolutely into the rain, heading for the engraver's shop. Jean-Marie sought refuge in the air, the rain and the long walk.

By the time he reached Louise's shop, the drizzle had become a downpour. He sought shelter under the overhang of an establishment across the street from Louise's shop, tightened his hat, and pulled up his collar. As the raindrops fell in rhythm, drip, drip, dripping off the overhang above him, he thought to himself, "Raindrops are so sad. They are like the sad beating of my heart. Perhaps someday, somebody will write a melody about raindrops. But it will have to be the tap, tap, tapping of piano keys to imitate the rhythm of these raindrops which drip so steadily from these eaves tonight. My violin does not have the nature to imitate raindrops, not like the piano does."

"Yes," thought Leclair sadly, "It will have to be a pianist in some distant future who has the delicate touch and the talent to write a prelude that captures the rhythm and deep sadness that I feel tonight in these raindrops."

He stared at the light in the shop. Louise must be in. The attraction of finding consolation in her face, a word of sympathy in her voice, a look in her eyes, to see her lovely dimples spring to life in her cheeks, was like a magnet. He resisted. He held himself back; he could not ring. He walked ponderously back to his wife in the pouring rain. Somehow, he did not notice that when he left his little shelter, the sign above the overhang read, "Maison Funéraire". By the time he got back to the apartment, his wife lay peacefully dead. He cried with her hand in his. "In a way," he thought, "it was a good thing we did not have children."

Thus, sadly, in 1728, in Paris, the week before Easter, his wife of 12 years passed away. It was a small funeral, carried out quickly and sadly. Again, it was a rainy day, with overcast clouds which perhaps mirrored how the spirit of Marie-Rose must have felt somewhere up in the sky, as it made its way into Heaven. Jean-Marie took the carriage home, sipped a glass of wine in the empty apartment to relax, and then made a sudden decision. It came like a bolt of lightning.

"The hell with it," he thought. He hailed another carriage and instructed the driver to go to Mme. Roussel's engraving shop. She noticed him coming and opened the door for him. "I saw you coming," she said, all smiles and dimples. He shook off his wet cape and hung it on the coatrack. "You are lucky," she said, "I am alone. I had no work for my assistant today". She led him to the back room. "A glass of wine? And let's get you warm".

Chapter 17

The wife dies

Jean-Marie was not a grieving bachelor after Marie-Rose died in 1728. It was accepted or rather ignored that men of a certain status and talent had affairs. Women apparently had to put up with that, and perhaps some of them had affairs too, all accepted as the way society ran and "the way of the world". This was a "modus vivendi" in some cultures, especially the French since it was considered as "libertine" by European standards. The only thing which could be said about Jean-Marie was that he held out until his wife, at least, passed away before he did anything openly about his desire for Louise.

Celibate was not a word Jean-Marie was familiar with after the age of 18. At least, he had kept his wedding vow to Marie-Rose until that Easter weekend. He knew the word loyalty while she was sick. No, he did not want to stab her in the back in a clandestine affair with Louise, while his wife was still alive. That kind of cad, he was not! And yet, if only his private thoughts could be read, and if one could look behind the scenes of his secret life, one could weave quite a story for the coffeehouses and tabloids of 18th century France!

Leclair was all of 31 years old at the time, and being a ballet dancer, he was quite fit, and he felt a need for a lover, a second wife perhaps, or both.

Louise shared a glass of wine with Jean-Marie in the back room as they held hands by the fire. He warmed up, and she comforted him in a way she always had wanted to. She put her hand on his thigh. They embraced. They agreed that for now, "this friendship with benefits", as they called it, would have to do. Some of the consideration was, of course, what society would think so soon after his wife's death. Public appearance was important. The other consideration was that each brought business and money into the relationship. Louise liked her independence. She had inherited the engraving business from her father, did quite well at it, and was proud to make it her own.

Jean-Marie and Louise Roussel were happy with their understanding. They "visited" each weekend, during the off hours, at the engraving studio. Meanwhile, Jean-Marie's music spread in popularity in the courts of the rich and famous.

Jean-Marie settled down to a new routine and in a strange way grew content now that Marie-Rose was no longer in his life. Jean-Marie got a dog, a little Shih Tzu puppy. At first, he was in a quandary as to what to name him. Lully. Rameau? Lully was dead so he might not mind. Rameau was still alive and that could be an insult. "Ah," Jean-Marie had an idea, "I will name the little scoundrel 'Monteverdi'."

"It will be a long name for a short little dog. How fitting!"

The dog seemed to be somewhat musical. He would sit and remain silent and sway when Jean-Marie practiced his sonatas in the room. "Yes, he has music in him," thought Jean-Marie. "This is a perfect match made in Heaven." A friend suggested that the dog's swaying was merely caused by the eyes of the dog following Jean-Marie's bow arm. But Jean-Marie preferred to think otherwise. "No, no, Monteverdi has the music in him!"

"Next you'll say he has perfect pitch too," said his friend.

"Why? Yes, he does!" asserted Jean-Marie.

"Never mind. I won't ask," said his friend.

John Hartig   Two Baroque Prodigies

That friend, of course, was Jean-Pierre Guignon. Both he and Jean-Marie had been advanced students of the great virtuoso and composer, Giovanni Battista Somis, when both of them lived in Turin. Somis still has a street named after him in Turin, "Via Giovanni Somis". The provenance, as it were, went back to Arcangelo Corelli, because Somis was a pupil of that great Italian master.

When Jean-Marie moved back to Paris he looked Guignon up. They had never really been close friends, but Jean-Marie made it a point of courtesy to drop in on him, and talk "old times" about their common mentor in the violin. So they visited and occasionally talked gossip at Jean-Marie's apartment once the wife died. That is when Jean-Marie introduced Monteverdi, his dog whom he was convinced had exceptional musical talents "beyond your average canine".

In the meantime, the dog, loosely called "Monte", on occasion, was getting so attached to Jean-Marie that he sat obediently at his feet while the master played or composed. "Monte" would only interrupt with a growl or give one bark for the signal that it was time for a walk, or if he needed to be fed, which the master would sometimes forget, if he was entranced in the middle of a musical phrase which needed putting down on paper.

"So, let's go out for your walk!" said Jean-Marie. The dog immediately perked up, seeming to understand the word, "Promenade." He looked upon his master with gleaming and adoring eyes. If the day were on a weekend, Jean-Marie ventured to walk the dog all the way to the engraving studio for a little afternoon delight.

In those days, carrying along a doggy-"do-do" bag was unheard of in France. Not until some 260 years later when France tried to clean up its act to make a clean impression internationally when Barcelona, Spain, a next-door neighbour, hosted the XXV Olympiad in 1992.

But in the old days, right up to the 20th century, dogs ran free, and when they had to go, they simply had to go, either to a bush, a tree, a lamppost, or sometimes in the middle of the street! When you are dealing with cobble stones, then the sticky stuff could get caught in all the nooks and crannies and remain there for days until it dried up and or was washed away by a good rain.

A person always had to walk with alertness underfoot in Paris, otherwise come home with doggy evidence stuck to one's shoes, and the chore of scraping things off with a stick before going indoors. With France's liberated attitude toward dogs, the country earned an international reputation among other nations as being a dirty country, especially on its streets. If you wanted to visit France, you had to watch out where you tread, and carry a big stick, not exactly in the meaning that Theodore Roosevelt intended!

Lampposts were Monteverdi's favourite repository or depository, whichever you prefer. Jean-Marie would look at the sky as if for musical inspiration while the dog went. He was glad that it was too early for the lamplighter to do his evening rounds, so the lamplighter would not notice what Monteverdi was doing.

Arguments could fly, if the lamplighter saw his beloved lamppost soiled upon and disrespected. And that occasionally happened too, whenever Jean-Marie took Monteverdi out for a brief nightly walk. Jean-Marie did not like a nightly encounter with the lamplighter. The lamplighter did not understand that a dog had to do his nightly rounds too! "If the man was that picky," thought Jean-Marie, "let him clean it up." Otherwise, Parisians relied on a good downpour of rain and the passage of time to solve the problem.

Both the dog and the composer loved their regular routines. The dog felt good, and the master got inspired.

Jean-Marie and Louise did not always transact their business in a slam-bam fashion. They shared feelings and often talked. He explained to her one time, "When I see a blank manuscript page, I want to fill it." He said he experienced the same thing when he read the lyrics of a poem to himself. They would go through his head like a song, like music straight from God.

Occasionally, he thought about what he would do when he got older, having lived with an older wife for years. "I'd probably keep on doing the same thing," he confessed. "I will never retire. I'm too busy for that." He was happy that his old friend in Turin, Somis, had advised him years ago to give up dancing and to concentrate his talent on playing the violin and on composing music.

"The music is in me," he said to Louise during a private moment, "I do realize that I am blessed." Then he quipped light-heartedly, "Sure beats ditch-digging!"

He added more seriously, "No, I would rather die than have the music in me ever stop." He didn't think about the prophetic truth in this that the day he died would be the day that the music died!

What he meant was that his life would be meaningless without music. He, along with gifted composers of his day, believed that music floated everywhere in the air, free for the taking, if you were sensitive enough to hear and feel it. His competitor, Phillipe Rameau, a composer who was 14 years his senior, also felt that we are the receptors of this music of the spheres, that was floating out there for sensitive souls to take for free!

Jean-Marie also believed like Rameau that God was in everything and everywhere, not like some invisible white bearded Father in the clouds interceding on behalf of his creation. Deism was a belief that once God created creation, he did not interfere, which appealed to Jean-Marie, Rameau and also Voltaire's sense of Reason. Many intellectuals of the 18th century thought that this type of God made more sense than the God of intercession preached by the Catholic Church. One could argue that this line of thinking, of a non-interfering God, appealed more to intellectuals because they were naturally more cynical.

*****

After Marie-Rose died, Jean-Marie promised himself he would visit Turin once a year and renew his friendship there with Giovanni Battista Somis. His former mentor was also older than he was, like Rameau, but only 11 years older. Jean-Marie thought of him like an older brother, valuing his advice. After Jean-Marie struck up his arrangement with Louise Roussel, Somis said to him, "You have to watch out for her. She is ambitious, she has a career, and she knows her mind. If the woman is too aggressive, she is a woman of experience, not only in business but also in sexual matters." Somis was cautioning his former pupil about his sleeping partners, "now that you are a free man again".

"Gonorrhoea and syphilis were a common side effect of a libertine lifestyle and a hazard among artists," he warned. "Zealous lovemaking with too many people can make you go blind," said Somis, "and I'm not kidding." Jean-Marie breathed a sigh of relief because so far, so good, he had had no symptoms of burning while urinating.

John Hartig   Two Baroque Prodigies

"Louise Roussel," he said, "isn't that kind of girl." So, when Jean-Marie went back to Paris, he resumed his walks with his dog, Monteverdi, and a confident friendship with Louise, "with benefits".

Chapter 18

Louise Roussel and Leclair

Louise Roussel and Jean-Marie did not have a respectable relationship, certainly not in respectable society, and certainly not in the eyes of the Catholic Church. It was a clandestine affair, as all such affairs needed to be in proper society, for having a mistress or a lover had its own code of ethics, and as long as it was not talked about, it could claim a private sense of decorum of its own. Such things among polite society could be tacitly tolerated, as long as everybody pretended it was secret. Now, that two and a half years had passed by since the death of his first wife, Jean-Marie and Louise had the social sanction to bring their relationship out into the open, since so much time had passed by, provided of course, they had the blessing of holy matrimony.

There was no rush, not even a thought, at first, about marrying each other. Their friendship "with benefits" was convenient and assured their independence because they each brought money into the union. Jean-Marie quite enjoyed his long walks with his little dog, Monteverdi, on Saturday afternoons when the "Closed" sign was on the outside door of the engraving shop. These walks were regular like clockwork. Monteverdi was given a bone to chew outside the back room of the shop and remained quiet knowing his master was on the other side of the door, moaning and groaning or whatever he was doing. Sex was not all there was to the affair; however, they often talked like friends, like lovers do.

"Why didn't you make a move on me earlier?" Louise asked one afternoon.

John Hartig   Two Baroque Prodigies

Louise spoke as a woman of her time, as a woman raised in the 18th century. She had always seen men as the aggressors. She wasn't shy herself about what she wanted, but she wanted to know why he didn't make a move. "I was waiting for you. After all, it's always been that way, hasn't it?"

"I suppose," said Jean-Marie stroking her hair while she lay on his shoulder. "But I could not be unfaithful to my sick wife at the time. It would have been like stabbing her in the back, secretly sneaking around when she was sick, when she was dying. I simply could not live with myself." Louise kissed him on the forehead.

"Have we found a magical island now?" she asked him.

"I don't think so. There are magical islands where we make money, when there are no wars, when we are healthy and strong, when we have new lovers...but no, there are no permanent magical islands. If there are, then I think, they are surrounded by the fires of hell, and we are lucky when those fires die down a bit even for a little time."

"That is cynical, Jean-Marie," she poked him.

"You want the truth or a wished-for dream?" he asked. "I do understand that we all have a need to escape the drudgery and pain of life...there is so much of it out there."

"So sad," she said, "like the dark clouds I feel gathering around Paris this late afternoon. Perhaps you want to stay the night?" Her actual living quarters were upstairs above the engraving shop.

"It's an agreeable idea," he conceded, snuggling closer. The dog snuffled outside the door. Jean-Marie opened the door and threw him another treat. He was glad he brought plenty of treats this afternoon. Monteverdi could bark so loudly out of tune when he was unhappy.

There was also something else that the couple was equipped with, in plenty of supply. Condoms. It was agreed that Jean-Marie would bring his own, and he had plenty extra for tonight, in fact plenty extra for every visit.

Condoms in the 18th century were available in a variety of qualities and sizes. They were either linen treated with spermicidal chemicals or "skin", made of bladder or intestine softened by treatment with sulphur and lye. France was a rather open society about sex and what goes on in people's lives. So, condoms were sold at pubs, barbershops, chemist shops, open-air markets, and at the theatre throughout Europe and Russia. Casanova in the 18th century was very innovative for his time period by using "assurance caps" to prevent impregnating his lovers. Jean-Marie was no Casanova, but he knew how to use a condom.

As double insurance, Louise kept diaphragms and spermicidal douches by her bedside upstairs with a ready supply of creams, gels, film, foams and suppositories. She knew how to use them and kept a few supplies downstairs in the cupboard of the back room, in case of spontaneous lovemaking.

Historically, birth control was always the woman's responsibility, not a fair fact, but it was so. In their affair, Jean-Marie bore some of the responsibility by bringing condoms for his afternoon's pleasure. The least he could do.

The problem with sex is, especially if you talk, share feelings and stay the night, is that you become bonded. That means you identify in things beyond sex, and one can call that love. That bonding occurred between Jean-Marie and Louise over the two and a half years in which they had their secret affair. One New Year Eve went by 1729 and then another in 1730.

John Hartig   Two Baroque Prodigies

New Year in France was celebrated more than Christmas in the 18th century. While the public celebrated the New Year with food and drink and family, Jean-Marie and Louise spent December 31, known as "la Saint Sylvestre", hunkered down in quiet seclusion within the confines of the upstairs rooms of the engraving shop. Louise missed not celebrating the feast with the rest of her larger family.

"You know," she confided during New Year's Eve of 1730, over a glass of wine, "it would be great to have other family come over to the shop next Saint Sylvestre and celebrate with us openly." This was as clear a hint about marriage she could muster for her lover of two years. Jean-Marie stared at her, "Let me think about it." He kissed her deeply, drank some wine, and said, "Let's have more cake before the midnight hour strikes at Notre Dame." The impressive Emmanuel bell that dates from the 1600s rung out its ringing across Paris as the couple toasted good fortune to each other for the following year January 1, 1730. "Perhaps family will come over next year," thought Louise, "with all her heart, and I can bring Jean-Marie out in the open. Maybe he will play the fiddle for us to bring in another year then."

The wedding took place on September 8, 1730. Jean-Marie Leclair was 33 years old. It was now two and a half years after the death of Jean-Marie's first wife. Louise and Jean-Marie felt they had waited long enough. The match seemed to be made more in heaven than with his older first wife, after all Louise was three years younger than Jean-Marie, and she had blue eyes, a pretty face and dimples which could light up a room.

New Year 1731 went as expected. It was indeed the best New Year that either one of them had ever celebrated. The larger family came over to the shop.

Everyone felt in a festive mood and brought food and drink. They patted Jean-Marie on the shoulder as they entered; embraced him and kissed him on both cheeks in the traditional French greeting. They brought their food and drink to the table already laid out with plates and cutlery. He was one of the family.

They took their plates and made a beeline for the breads, cheeses, meats, paté, oysters, and foie gras. They drank wine and champagne, and told jokes, some of them rife and ribald. Soon Uncle Gaston, the first to finish his multi-course menu, hors-d'oeuvre, soup and entrée, ignored the fish and sorbet and eyed the desserts with a child's delight: pot de crème, crêpes, opera cake, custard tart, poire belle hélène, and the box of cherry chocolates. As the evening went on with the initial food and drink, they urged Jean-Marie to play something. He joked that he would not play the violin that evening, but the fiddle, treating his new family to traditional French folk tunes. Uncle Gaston teased Jean-Marie that he would specifically save a piece of "opera cake" for the august violinist in the group. "I will hold you to that," joked Jean-Marie, patting Uncle Gaston's ample tummy.

At midnight, the bells in the towers of Notre Dame rung out that Saint Sylvestre. New Year had arrived, 1731! Louise was so happy. Jean-Marie was red cheeked and smiling broadly from all the drinking and playing he did. They were not only celebrating a New Year but a new life together. Jean-Marie was 34, and Louise was 31.

Chapter 19

The King's Court

The marriage, and Jean-Marie's career, seemed to go splendidly for at least 3 years, at most 5 years. You can safely say several years of happiness. Louise had her steady job printing her husband's compositions and those of other musicians, plus there were the engravings and prints of various artworks. Jean-Marie had his pension from his patron, the financier, M. Bonnier de la Mosson, as well as the remuneration he received from his performances in the city's concert series. The couple continued to enjoy life, each other and success. But like the Parisian weather, there was always a cloud in the silver lining.

First, a spark of good fortune! In 1733, Jean-Marie was named "ordinaire de la musique" by Louis XV, quite an honour from the King's orchestra. Then, in 1734 he was appointed "Premier Symphoniste du Roy", not a bad title for the son of a haberdasher. That meant he was now concert master of the orchestra.

Well, the honour had to be recognized, especially when you get such a title from King Louis XV. In gratitude, Jean-Marie Leclair dedicated his set of sonatas to the monarch [one source says Third Book set, another source says Opus 5 set]. Whatever you call it, the Third Book was a milestone for violin virtuosi of all levels, perhaps similar to Paganini's Capriccios. Sere de Rieux made a note about the importance of the Third Book: "Leclair is the first composer who, imitating nothing, has created something fine and new, something that is distinctively his own."

King Louis XV called his first violinist into court one day and presented him with a gold-plated pocket watch which had the King's image and coat of arms engraved on the inside. Jean-Marie bowed with delight and proudly retreated from the King's presence. "I shall keep this forever," he thought.

This was all fine, if Jean-Marie Leclair were the only rooster in the hen house, but an old acquaintance of his soon flexed his musical muscles, Jean-Pierre Guignon, who had his eye on the top spot. Threateningly, the man had talent! He, like Jean-Marie, had been a personal violin pupil of the great Giovanni Battista Somis back in Turin in the old days.

Both Jean-Marie Leclair and Jean-Pierre Guignon competed for public acclaim and notice from the King. They both performed in the King's orchestra, as well as the "Concert Spirituel", the city's concert series.

Similar to the earlier musical jousting between Locatelli and Jean-Marie, which was fun, Jean-Marie and Guignon squared off, but in earnest, during the concert series to show who was the best violinist! M. Marc Pincherie was an eyewitness, reporting that there was no clear victory. "Their performing styles differed profoundly, Leclair's being more precise, more technically delicate, more cerebral, while Guignon's was more colourful, more fanciful." It should be noted here that references in various sources about Guignon's name vary in spelling, sometimes found as, Guignon. Perhaps the variation is due to his original Italian name being Frenchified. Guignon did become a French citizen, however.

Historical footnotes aside, the two couldn't stand each other. Louise, at home, noticed that her husband was growing moodier and more withdrawn by 1736. This musical animosity had also been brought to the attention of the King.

An aide, who knows all and hears all, told Louis XV that certain sparks were flying between the two violinists both in the Chapelle and in the Chambre du Roi. The King agreed that perhaps the competition could be settled with a compromise, so that the two men could take turns being concert master.

"Your Highness," said the aide, "how can two grown men be so childish?"

"Well," said the King, "you should see some of my elder statesmen!"

"Then, who shall take the first turn as first violin?"

"How about a toss of the coin?" suggested the King.

"Your Majesty, if you permit, I have an old souvenir, a Louis d'or, from the old days..." said the aide.

"No, no, you keep your souvenir," commanded the King, "let us use my own coin, minted just last year, a silver Écu of myself. You call it, heads or tails. Heads is for Leclair going first for first." His Royal Majesty chuckled at his little quip.

"Heads," said the aide, "your image is so imposing whenever it comes up."

The King flipped the coin, caught it and put it on the back of his other hand. It was heads indeed, with the regal head of His Majesty staring out into destiny. "Jean-Marie will be first violin this month! So be it!"

"But" asked the aide, "is there a permanent solution? To whom should the first violin honour go then?"

The King said, "To the strongest." He added, "Let them play it out to the end...and I do not mean the music!" The King chuckled and smiled with amusement, enjoying the personal drama among his staff. He enjoyed toying with them.

The other members of the orchestra did not enjoy the tension between the two men, and some of them did not know which one of them to follow when they were playing. The music suffered. Perhaps the King did not care. His enjoyment was personal drama and the court gossip. But all that did not matter, because Jean-Marie Leclair had had enough by 1736.

When Guignon's turn came the next month to be concert master, Jean-Marie was damned if he was going to take lead instruction from this second fiddle. He packed up his violin, walked out of the rehearsal and resigned from the King's service. He never performed in the public concert series again at the "Concert Spirituel". His pupils, however, continued to play there and perhaps were a living legacy there to the teaching skills of their volatile violin teacher. According to one source, their names were Pierre Gavinies and L'Abbe le Fils.

*****

Jean-Marie was sending out feelers for work outside of France. His home life was also in shambles, falling apart not only because of friction at work, but because of rising personal matters involving his wife, Louise.

As to the man's virtuosic abilities, historians are inclined to compare him with Bach, or certainly musicians above Guignon's caliber. Perhaps he wasn't as great a giant as Bach, but nevertheless the man was great. He needed and wanted respect for his talent. Musicians worldwide recognize him for his musical sophistication, his knowledge of harmonies and orchestral writing.

Jean-Marie Leclair is played world-wide in modern times by people no less than, Itzhak Perlman and Pinchas Zukerman accompanying the piano in a Trio by Jean-Marie

John Hartig   Two Baroque Prodigies

Leclair, Sonata No. 5, or virtuoso Henryk Szeryng playing the Leclair violin Sonata in D major, Opus 3 No. 3. Where is Jean-Pierre Guignon in all this? He remained a musical glimmer in history, whereas Jean-Marie Leclair became a star.

Francois Filiatrault, went so far as to say, "We are tempted to call him, for the technical power of his skills, the French Bach."

Chapter 20

Rocky Marriage

The private lives of Louise Roussel and Jean-Marie Leclair are difficult to pin down in terms of what exactly happened there and when. We know that by 1734, Jean-Marie was living on the Rue Saint Benoit, near the Abaie Saint Germain. That obviously meant he had moved out of the house and gotten himself a new location away from his wife's engraving shop.

It's always sad when a loving relationship disintegrates, sometimes the fault of circumstances, clashing personalities, strains about career and money, and sometimes nobody's fault, where you just fall out of love. Maybe with them it was all of the above, ending with falling out of love, but maybe never not quite!

The first sign of bad things to come came with the dog's death. Shortly after Jean-Marie was named "ordinaire de la musique" by the King in 1733, Louise forgot to close the door to the shop and inadvertently let the dog out. Monteverdi scampered out into the street at the exact moment that a speeding carriage passed by hitting the poor little dog with a wheel crushing its poor little chest. Monteverdi gave out one yelp and then expired. Jean-Marie was angry with his wife. They found a little piece of earth in the back yard by a tree to bury their musical hound in. No matter how many times she apologized for her carelessness, Jean-Marie turned away from her and sulked.

Things improved, however, when Jean-Marie was made "Premier Symphoniste du Roy" the following year in 1734. But after that lush appointment, tensions at work in the orchestra mounted. Guignon made suggestions about the choices of music and even criticized Leclair's dynamics.

Jean-Marie exhibited irritable moods during rehearsal times, and he took those feelings home to his wife. He sulked and occasionally said snippy things. They just came out; he didn't mean them. She retreated to her work in the back of the shop. On his part, he had found a private studio somewhere in Paris where he could saw away at his fiddle to work off his frustrations.

It's not exactly clear when little Louise was conceived or finally born, but sometime during this difficult period, Louise Roussel took on the big-bellied look of pregnancy. Jean-Marie was furious. He was not in the mood to be a father. "I thought we agreed that our careers would come first. That our careers were the only thing. You had all your contraceptives to prevent a pregnancy. What went wrong? Or was this deliberate?" This crushed Louise.

Jean-Marie relented somewhat, and in a spirit of compromise said, "Fine, if it's a boy, it will be fine." He was hoping that a son would mean a legacy where he could teach the boy all he knew about the violin. "But", he threatened, "if it's a girl, I'm divorcing you." They stopped sleeping together from that point forward, and he moved out of the house into his own little apartment. "Been there, done that," he thought to himself, sipping a glass of wine late at night. This time he had no little Monteverdi to console him through his lonely nights. Occasionally he picked up a lady of the night if he had the urge to be with somebody. He remembered to use his condom or "assurance cap". Those were used primarily, not for contraception, but to prevent catching a sexually transmitted disease.

When the baby came, it was a girl. Louise named her, Louise. She too became an engraver like her mother. She had no inclination towards music, and if she did, it was not encouraged by the mother. Louise fashioned the little girl into a miniature of herself. When she grew up, she married a painter. Jean-Marie had nothing to do with the girl.

And so, Jean-Marie opened the page to a different chapter in his life. He closed the book on his life with Louise. It was him and his violin against the world.

By 1737, Jean-Marie was 40 years old, and Louise was 37. The Little Sparrow was still energetic, quick in her movements, and still looked pretty with those blue eyes and dimples, despite some facial lines. Jean-Marie was getting a furrow in the forehead and a little paunch around the tummy.

Now that reality faced him, Jean-Leclair dragged his feet about a divorce. In fact, it didn't happen until 1758, in another 21 years!

It is difficult to say why they let this action go on so long. Maybe, it was out of apathy, no respect for government documentation; maybe it came from a little lifeline for not letting go, holding on to someone you once loved?

It took 21 long years, and by that time, Jean-Marie was 61 years old, and Louise was 58 when they finally divorced. Both of them were white haired, walked with a stoop, and facially, they were getting wrinkled.

Although they drifted apart, mostly because of circumstances and understandable tensions at work, they were never really spiteful towards each other during all this mess, after Monteverdi died and even while that battle was going on with that insufferable Guignon. They certainly were not enemies. Even after Jean-Marie moved out, they found ways of working together because they were still tied by business interests, and they somehow respected the affectionate history they had together at one time.

Louise Roussel published and printed Jean-Marie's compositions from Opus 2 onward. There was a total of 92 works published. Many for violin as well as several theatrical productions, including Opus 15 and one opera. Strangely enough, despite their personal clashes after Monteverdi died, Louise and Jean-Marie reached a civilized agreement where her business would still publish all his works, even after their separation.

But perhaps the slowly festering problem lay in the fact that both of them were such high-strung people, stuck in and married to very demanding careers. There was no room for children, at least not on his side. How ironic, he coming from a family of 7 siblings, although one source says 6 siblings.

Chapter 21

The Rolling Stone
As early as 1734, Jean-Marie was sending out letters of introduction to various courts and heads of state throughout Europe, not being happy with his working environment at the Chapelle and in the Chambre du Roi, especially with Guignon there. Haydn apparently made a remark, something to the effect, where Mozart is, there Haydn cannot be. But that was praise from a friend, nothing like what Leclair and Guignon experienced when they were occupying the same space together.

It was also strange how the death of Monteverdi, his little dog, poisoned Leclair's home life. He just wouldn't let it go, blaming his wife.

So, letters went out to various nobility and to fellow musicians alike throughout Europe, as early as 1734, letting it be known that Jean-Marie Leclair was looking for work outside of France. It's always a clever idea to send out "résumés" and letters of introductions, while still employed at home, especially under unfavourable conditions.

By 1737, Jean-Marie Leclair received an envelope with the royal seal of the Princess of Orange on it, from Leeuwarden. He would receive a warm welcome there.

He started packing: a huge trunk with clothes and all his worldly possessions. He would carry his precious violin in his arms. He had a comforter for his knees to rest his violin upon. He would be leaving on the 5:00 a.m. stagecoach which would head out of the City of Light, facing a 10-day rough ride ahead, first into northern France, then further north yet through Belgium and finally, if no wheel broke

John Hartig   Two Baroque Prodigies

on the coach or a horse died, onto to the Netherlands and Leeuwarden.

The coach would be stopping overnight at various inns. He could sight-see by sliding back the shutters in the windows of the coach, but then he would have to cover his mouth with his handkerchief because of the dust or wear a bandana.

Jean-Leclair was 40 years old and still robust enough to make such a journey, unlike Mozart's mother who some four decades later was so stressed out by travel and a strange city, she got sick and died at the age of 37. That strange city was Paris. Mozart knew little French. Leclair was fortunate enough to be fluently multi-lingual, and not so coddled by his parents in his formative years. In that respect, Leclair was a survivor and looked forward to the adventure of going to the Netherlands, all 540 kilometers to get there, better than a week-long trip, maybe 10 or 11 days. Unlike the Mozarts who travelled as a family, Leclair travelled as a single man, was still robust and also had money.

The stops were roughly evenly spaced, staying over at local inns for food and drink, and a good night's rest. The coach averaged about 50 kilometres per day, before they stopped at an inn for nourishment and sleep. The only cities of any note were Arras, on the second day, Lille, the last stop in northern France on the third day, then some unknown inn in some unknown town on the fourth day, then on to Ghent the fifth day, Antwerp on the sixth, some unknown inn and town on the seventh day [probably St. Annbosch], avoid the side trip to Rotterdam and The Hague, stop in Utrecht on the eighth or ninth day, avoid the side trip to Amsterdam, stay in an unknown inn and unknown town on the ninth or tenth day, and finally kick the dust off the coach at Leeuwarden either on the tenth or eleventh day.

The schedule in 1737 was not rigid, depending upon rest for the horses and passengers, also the road conditions, weather and mechanical problems like broken wheels.

Leclair looked forward to Arras on the second day, because the city was known for its architecture and its history. It was once part of the Spanish Netherlands. He looked forward to tasting its wine. Lille was nothing to speak of, but it was the most northern town before the coach got to Belgium. When they got to the border, Leclair enjoyed the look of the peaceful countryside. Belgium was known for its laid-back culture and its peace.

Heinrich Heine, the 19th century German poet and philosopher, reflected upon the nature of Belgium. He is reported to have said, "When the world ends, I will go to Belgium. There everything happens 50 years later." He also said with keen insight, "Where they burn books, they will, in the end, burn human beings too." He didn't know he was talking about his own country, Germany. But then Heinrich Heine was a German Jew and a visionary.

Jean-Marie Leclair did not know any of these things, either Heinrich Heine's sayings or the Weltschmerz of the Romantic poets. He merely looked out the window of his carriage when they got to Belgium and dreamed.

They should reach Ghent on the fifth day, the city known for its luxury clothes, and Leclair hoped great wine. Antwerp was on the itinerary for the sixth day, the city of finance and the diamond trade. Surely, there had to be good wine there! The seventh day meant another unknown inn in another unknown town.

The coach would bring Leclair to Utrecht and finally the Netherlands. Utrecht meant architecture again, stretching

John Hartig   Two Baroque Prodigies

back to the High Middle Ages. The Treaty of Utrecht brought an end to the War of the Spanish Succession in 1713 between England and France. France was driven out of the Spanish Netherlands by this treaty, not a happy deal for King Louis XIV, the Sun King. Surely the town too had good wine!

The coach avoided Amsterdam. Leclair did not care for the art and architecture there. They drove on for the ninth and tenth days, stopping overnight at little towns. The food was good, as was the wine, and the bed was passable, without bugs. On the eleventh day, the coach drove into Leeuwarden, close to the northern coast of Holland.

What an adventure! A friend told Leclair, "As long as you keep your sphincter tight, you should be doing fine on the trip." They laughed at that. Leclair asked, "Is it true if you ain't Dutch, you ain't much?" There must have been some jocular equivalent to that saying in French at the time, pointing out the attitude of superiority one nation or race seemed to have over others. That was human nature!

Territorial identities, even within a country, were strong in the 18th century. Wars were fought on that basis. Leeuwarden was also known as Stadsfries, or the capital of Friesland within the Netherlands. It was also Protestant, welcoming Jean-Marie Leclair, a non-practicing Catholic from a Roman Catholic France. Even though Leclair was a Deist, he had no place in his life for religion, period! His religion was his violin.

Nothing is said about the origin of his violin, so it might as well have been a Stradivarius. He won it in Turin when his mentor Somis set up a violin competition at the Turin Opera. The two physical possessions which Leclair valued the most were, first his violin, and secondly, his gold pocket watch from King Louis XV. He kept his gold pocket watch safely tucked away in his big trunk for the trip, thinking that was safer than in his vest pocket if a road agent stopped the coach.

He told a friend once, "I wish I could wave a wand and turn all guns into violins. They would make a better sound than the gunpowder that takes a life."

Jean-Marie Leclair did not know it, but he soon found out that the Princess of Orange had problems of her own. He wondered if he had walked from one hornet's nest in Paris into another hornet's nest in Leeuwarden. Maybe all royal courts were the same?

His welcome was indeed warm. The Princess was not available at the moment, but her aide ushered Leclair in to have food and drink. He even offered Leclair an anteroom in which he could practice his violin before he entertained the Princess with his talent. Leclair had a slice of baguette with cheese and meat, a bit of wine, and then retired to the anteroom with his violin to warm up his playing. Even in the little room, the sound of his arpeggios and then his launch into one of his own concerti echoed out into the hallway. A servant passed by, mesmerized, and slipped the door of the anteroom slightly ajar.

"Sir," he asked, "you are playing without any music in front of you. Do you not read notes?"

Leclair chuckled and responded in perfect Dutch, "Read notes? No, not enough to hurt my music any." The servant soon learned that the very opposite was true. Jean-Marie Leclair did more than read notes. He could write them on paper, and he could make them up in his head wherever he would go.

He was pleased when he was introduced at court to her Royal Highness, the Princess of Orange. She was intelligent and loved music. She spoke German, French and English, as did Leclair. She was also adept at singing and the harpsichord. In fact, her teacher had been none other than Georg Friedrich Handel. Handel disdained teaching, and thought it was a mundane chore, but he said that he would make one exception, and that was for Anne, "the flower of princesses." The Princess of Orange remained a lifelong supporter of Handel's.

It was ironic that Anne and King Louis XV of France at one point had been considered potential marriage partners, but the idea was soon discarded when the French nobility insisted that Anne convert to Catholicism. Instead, she married William IV, Prince of Orange, who had a spinal deformity. She was afraid that she would remain a spinster for the rest of her life, especially since smallpox had ruined her looks when she was a child. Her father and brother were opposed to her marrying William, but she retorted [something to the effect], "I'd rather marry him even if he were a baboon."

So, the royal family in the Netherlands had its own troubles into which Jean-Marie Leclair stepped unknowingly, as long as he was paid for doing what he loved to do, without a Guignon to deal with.

Employment in Holland lasted from 1737 until 1742, a total of 5 years. During that time, Leclair met Locatelli again, one source says in Amsterdam, and took violin lessons from him. The source comments that Leclair convinced Locatelli to move the publication of the concerti and caprices of his Arte del Violino to Paris. Who knows? Could Leclair have been drumming up business for his almost ex-wife?

At any rate, the Locatelli influence is shown in Leclair's Fourth Book of violin sonatas, Opus 9 dating from 1737 to 1738, as sure compliment to a friend. The dedication, however, for the Fourth Book went to Princess Anne of Orange. It is not clear how many times she received him officially at court; it could have been when he first arrived at Leeuwarden, and perhaps again at a later date. But other than snippets of names and dates in various histories, there is little known about Leclair's mysterious life in Holland.

Apparently, in 1740, he conducted the private orchestra of Francois du Liz, a very wealthy man, living in The Hague. As often happens with mad speculators, du Liz went bankrupt, so Leclair ended up in Paris in June 1743. But in keeping with his earlier relocations between Turin and Paris, he again did not stay long.

He is next traced to Chambery in the mountains of southeastern France where becomes a mentor to Don Filipe of Spain who liked to reside there. Like Frederick the Great of Prussia, Don Filipe was an amateur musician who would get up at 4:00 a.m. to practice his cello or the treble viol. If you had the wealth, you could get private lessons from the likes of Jean-Marie Leclair. In 1745, Leclair dedicated a second set of concerti to the Spanish Prince.

"Then back to Paris," says a source.

One would wonder what his life would have been like had Jean-Marie stayed in Paris with his wife all along and been a father to little Louise? One could hear a faint echo of a complaint, also coming from his first wife who had wanted to stay in Lyons years before, not wanting to bounce around between Turin and Paris. Jean-Marie Leclair was ever the rolling stone.

Like Frederick the Great and Johannes Joachim Quantz, Jean-Marie Leclair would have been better to remain a bachelor, especially after his first wife died. Who knew the traps he would get into with Louise Roussel?

Chapter 22

Male mid-life crisis

In 1745, Jean-Marie Leclair was 48 years old. He was back in Paris. We wonder if he dropped in to see his wife and daughter at this time. The couple was still not officially divorced after an 11-year separation, probably more. There are no letters revealing how Leclair's wife felt about her itinerant husband, which was probably resentment, bitterness, maybe even hatred? Would there have been some negative transference to the little girl? How would the daughter have felt not having a father there, a father who felt his fame was more important than his family, than her? Jean-Marie Leclair was like a pirate on a fast running sailing ship, cutting through the high seas, not caring whom he swamped or what damage he left behind in his wake. But onward he had to go to conquer new shores!

In 1746, Leclair composed his first operatic work, "Scylla and Glaucus". Actually, it was his one and only opera. He recently turned 50 and had high hopes for this new direction in his life, which did not quite pan out as he wanted. "Scylla and Glaucus" was staged at the Academie Royale de Musique on October 4. It was a lavish production and is noted as having been "politely" received.

The story came from Ovid's "Metamorphoses" where the beautiful Scylla falls in love with Glaucus, the sea god. But Circe, the witch, is jealous and turns Scylla into an ugly monster. One would wonder if Leclair transferred the jealousy and rivalry, he experienced personally with Guignon during his service to the King into the characters of Circe and Scylla? Perhaps his own deep hurt in the King's Symphony fired up the words Jean-Marie used in the lyrics for his opera?

If you take aging into account, one could argue that Jean-Marie's composing ability got less and less over the last two decades of his life. This would mean from the age of 44 on, roughly the time period in which we are concerned here. It is reported that Leclair even burned some manuscripts which did not satisfy him. Apparently, Brahms was the same way.

Perhaps Leclair was like a wild boar rooting for truffles and finding clumps of clay instead. Perhaps a genius's clumps of clay are other people's diamonds. Maybe word got out to friends that Leclair needed reassurance, a friendly hand at the time, to say, "Good job".

In 1748, when Leclair was 51, his former student Antoine-Antonin, who also happened to be a French nobleman, a Duke, specifically "le Duc de Gramont", was just that hand, that Leclair so desperately needed. It would make a good Ph.D. thesis to trace the self-esteem and the lack of confidence which strangely plagues some men of genius. The duke made Leclair principal violinist and director of his private orchestra at Puteaux. Again, like Francois du Liz, wealthy investor, or the Prince of Spain, wealthy royal patron, it helps to have money with which to buy your own private orchestra, as long as you remain solvent financially. Leclair had struck it rich several times with such wealthy men, but as many times, it seems, lost his job when they went bankrupt. The Duke of Gramont ended Leclair's employment as musical director in 1751 when he was forced to sell his Puteaux estate because of debts.

It is not clear whether Jean-Marie Leclair finally got an official divorce from Louise Roussel in 1758, or if he skipped the paperwork, and finally and permanently just moved out. Whatever the case, the disintegration of the marriage had been going on for years and it was a very tragic note in Jean-Marie Leclair's biography.

There could be a case made over the past two decades that Louise Roussel suffered from menopause, had no interest in sex, claimed it hurt, things which spiraled into other irritations in their lives. Enthusiasm in their jobs were tainted by needling and arguments around the supper table. Leclair imagined what life would be like again on his own. He yearned for independence as the 1750s drew to a close; he did not want to be tied to his wife's income.

They say, as you get older, you become more of what you always were, more stubborn if you were stubborn, more opinionated if you were opinionated. Leclair did not want to rely on the hospitality of friends. That is perhaps why he rejected the offer of hospitality made by his friend and former employer, the Duke of Gramont, when Leclair looked for another place to stay, away from his wife. 28 years of marriage just seemed to be thrown away. Leclair was 61 years old in 1758.

Perhaps similar to his wife's menopause, he, himself, was going through a male mid-life crisis. Perhaps, there was constant needling and a push on Louise's part for Leclair to succeed more as a composer and as a court favourite. Even though they might have had separate rooms in the upstairs of the engraving shop, she might have thrown comparisons in his face at the supper table, if they even ate together, "Look at Haydn, a younger man!" Leclair might have moved out and rented a small apartment further down the street from his wife to save his sanity. Louise apparently was also experiencing a financial downturn in her business around this time, perhaps as a result of the general family dysfunction.

By 1758, while Leclair moved all his belongings out of the upstairs of the engraving shop, Louise moved out too, and in with a stone and brick mason, named Monsieur Chavagnac. They had lodgings together in the Rue du Four-Saint-Germain. One would assume that living with a bricklayer, one could afford decent housing in Paris, a better situation than what Leclair chose for himself.

Leclair, for his part, chose to live in a hovel in the Rue de Careme-Prenant on the outskirts of northern Paris, in a notorious part of the city, called "Le Marais". A Ph.D. student could again investigate the psychological motivation here for a musical genius to deliberately live poorly in a demeaning way.

Leclair's patron, the Duke of Gramont, offered to take Leclair into his own home at this time, to house him on his property and perhaps feed him through his generous hospitality, rather than see his principal violinist live in an unsavoury part of town. Our Ph.D. student could also investigate why Leclair left Louise or vice versa in a study about genius psychosis. Maybe it all goes back to Monteverdi, the little dog, although now we are stretching it!

Leclair was no doubt stubborn and proud. Like a petulant child, he might have said, "I don't owe the world a thing; I can do it myself!" He preferred to live in a hovel for the last six years of his life out of pride, rather than live on a rich man's handout. Most likely if Leclair had accepted the duke's kind offer, he might have been able to pull his bootstraps up, and recover his dignity, and not been murdered in 1764. Who knows?

When he first bought the little hovel in 1758 from a Monsieur Legras, Jean-Marie did not really check into what he was getting. They say, "Buyer beware!" Perhaps the location should have told him everything, a small house close to Saint-Martin's canal. The canal district had a bad reputation for thieves, prostitutes and all manner of unsavoury people. He bought the house anyway, despite protestations from close friends, like the Duke of Gramont. This was his way of saying to Louise, "Look I own something of my own now; I don't need you." It may also have been a way to live the life of a miser or a bohemian, a deliberate choice, which said I don't need society or its demands to get ahead.

Jean-Marie Leclair sat alone one night in his chair in his little house on the Rue de Careme-Prenant with a blanket over his shoulders and contemplated his life in the dark. He stoked the fire in the little fireplace and shivered.

In the 18th century, people had to put up with draughty houses and fireplaces which were inefficient. A lot of heat escaped up the chimney and through ill-fitting windows. One could feel that especially in autumn and winter. Jean-Marie Leclair, despite his fame at one point in his life, and also some accumulated fortune, could not now afford the Franklin Stove, otherwise known as the "Pennsylvania fireplace" which was invented by Benjamin Franklin in 1740. It was basically a heating stove which didn't let all its heat escape up the chimney. Leclair would have to order one, pay for the import tax and shipping, and then, the installation in a house that wasn't worth it. This could be done if Leclair had enough money, but the expense was a very discouraging thought. So, Leclair shivered and drew his blanket tighter around himself.

He did not believe in God, but he feared Him. Leclair brushed his hand over his visage. Had he made a mistake in buying the house? Jean-Marie Leclair did not know anything about Cyrano de Bergerac, the play written much later in 1897, but he felt instinctively that his large nose meant he was destined for something great, and certainly better things than this. Even yet, it might not be too late! He shivered again, drew in his blanket tight around his shoulders, and stoked the fireplace. He had to talk with Monsieur Legras about fixing the leaky roof and the draughty windows better than he had the first time. He would have to pay the man extra money.

As one year dragged on to become six years in the little house, Leclair lost his health. He lost his suppleness which he had taken for granted as a young dancer years ago in Lyons. Once a beautiful dancer full of strength, he now felt his body had shrunk, and he had become a limping old man.

While Leclair's health of body and mind waned, Franz Joseph Haydn was on the rise, growing stronger and more famous. Born in 1732, Haydn became Vice-Kapellmeister of the Esterházy musical establishment in 1764. At the time, Haydn was 32 years old, and Leclair was 67 [and shortly, dead].

The two men had different temperaments. Leclair was a rolling stone and Haydn was content to stay put. Haydn had a steady job and was employed with the Esterházys for nearly 30 years. Did Haydn sit in a coffeehouse in Eisenstadt, Austria, in 1764 and talk about Leclair's ignominious demise? Did the Esterhazys even care about Leclair's death? Did they ask Haydn what he thought about the tragedy, except to gossip about it? Maybe neither Haydn nor the Esterhazys knew about the death or bothered to talk about it. Why should Franz Joseph Haydn be interested in a tottering old Frenchman who had had his time at fame and glory?

*****

John Hartig   Two Baroque Prodigies

But let's look at the last six years of Leclair's life and the direction it could or could not have gone. Let's put Leclair in a granny suite, let's say, on the property of the Duke of Gramont, if Leclair took up the duke's offer of hospitality. If the killer was indeed the nephew whom Leclair continuously rebuffed, then whether Leclair lived in the little hovel, or on the grounds of the Duke of Gramont, the end result would probably have been the same. Leclair would have been murdered! Somehow, the envious nephew would have found a way to get at his uncooperative and more talented uncle. If Leclair were living on the duke's estate, the nephew would have stood a better chance of getting caught; however, mainly because the nephew would have been trespassing on a rich man's property.

A dark little house in a shabby part of town stood little chance of having a witness or anybody caring. Especially if the house was located close to the canal.

So, in the early morning of October 23rd, 1764, Jean-Marie Leclair was found dead!

*****

Scholars agree that the nephew probably did it. They even tie the nephew and the ex-wife together in a conspiracy theory, saying that the nephew and the ex-wife conspired together to do Leclair in, one for revenge and the other for financial gain. There is even a far-fetched notion that the duke, himself, might have done the deed, although credence in such a claim is thin. The Duke of Gramont still had his nobleman's status and surely enough money, even if he had to sell Puteaux to pay various business or gambling debts. Why stoop so low from his status of nobility to kill a hired musician?

Indeed, it was a complicated case with only circumstantial, if no solid evidence, against the most likely of one or two suspects on the list. The killer was never accused or arrested, leaving behind inadvertently, a perfect crime? Data collection, investigative methodology and forensics, of course, were still in the dark ages as far as solving crimes was concerned. In the Leclair case, Police Lieutenant de Sardine and his trusty note taker, Gentilhomme, were the best the police force at that time could muster. It's too bad that no clear evidence brought no clear suspect to justice! It should also be noted that specifics were lacking about the wounds inflicted upon poor Leclair's body, whether he was stabbed 3 times in the back or one time in the neck and twice in the back. It seemed details like that did not matter in those days.

Chapter 23

It was not a good year

1764 was not a good year for composers. But then it's never a good year for composers when they die. There were Locatelli, Rameau and Leclair, a trio of big names of the Baroque era, who sadly passed away.

Pietro Antonio Locatelli died on March 30, 1764, in his house on the Prinsengracht in Holland. He had climbed the ladder of success, coming such a long way from Bergamo, his hometown in the alpine Lombardy region of northern Italy. He was 68 when he died, a year older than his friend, Jean-Marie Leclair. Then Rameau died just over half a year later on September 12 of that year, and Leclair himself died, stabbed to death, on October 23rd or October 24th.

When Locatelli died in the spring of 1764, there was enough time for the news to travel to the ears of both Rameau and Leclair that Locatelli, the great violin virtuoso had died in Holland. We wonder what their reaction was when they first heard the news that this fellow musician, a virtuosic violinist and composer like themselves, had passed away? Certainly, Leclair would have been personally affected because Locatelli was a friend, with whom he had at least two friendly musical jousts in a concert series.

The first friendly competition came shortly after 1728, once Leclair had settled in Paris. Leclair made a side trip to Kassel where the two virtuosi publicly performed in a "battle of the violins". The idea was to publicize the difference between the French and the Italian styles of playing. A witness described Leclair's playing as angelic, graced with a beautiful tone, and not restricted to rhythmic rules. Locatelli, on the other hand, played like the devil, aggressively hitting the strings with a deliberate edgy sound. The audience loved it and the two musicians became life-long friends.

This relationship was so different than what Leclair had with Jean-Pierre Guignon, a member of King Louis XV's Royal Symphony. Guignon and Leclair competed for the first violin position in the orchestra and could not stand each other's company. Perhaps it made some difference in that Locatelli and Leclair only met on occasion and did not live in the same city. Whereas Leclair and Guignon lived in Paris and played in the same concert series of the Concert Spirituel.

One other obvious factor is that the chemistry of personalities between the two men did not gel. They irritated each other and thought they were better players than others.

When Jean-Marie Leclair resigned from the King's orchestra in 1736, that left the field wide open for Guignon to slide over into the first violin chair in the King's court. Guignon must have been beaming with a smile as wide as the Cheshire cat's. Leclair in the meantime shook the dust off his feet in Paris and moved to Holland in 1737. Leclair was all of 39 years old at the time, maybe 40.

His job in Holland lasted 5 years from 1737-1442. He got reacquainted with Locatelli in Amsterdam. A biographical note says that Leclair took violin lessons from Locatelli. One wonders how Leclair managed to subdue his ego enough to take violin lessons, as a pupil, from Locatelli. Somehow their personalities clicked agreeably.

It wasn't like Locatelli didn't have an ego of his own. A certain bearing and even exaggerated flashiness was expected from performers of his caliber in those days on stage. When the Italian maestro was in Germany, he played before Frederick William I. An anecdotal report describes the maestro's self-assurance, and indeed his vanity, in wearing glitzy, diamond-studded clothes.

There are other questions which come to mind in the collaboration between Leclair and Locatelli. Locatelli seemed to be protective of the secrets of his violin technique. He would give lessons to amateurs but had a rule not to teach professionals. He feared that they would learn too many of his secrets, with the threat, perhaps, of becoming better than he? So, one wonders how Leclair convinced Locatelli to give him violin lessons, unless Locatelli made sure that what he taught his compeer was not everything about his violin technique.

People of wealth who professed to be amateur musicians flocked to Locatelli in Amsterdam to be taught by the great master. Locatelli grew rich. An amusing sidenote is that in 1741, he opened up shop, selling violin strings out of his home, perhaps a seemingly lowly business transaction, but it made him money. Combined with his income from his performances and his violin instruction, he soon had the highest income of any musician in all of Amsterdam.

Perhaps part of Leclair's problem was that he didn't stay in one place long enough to put down roots, and he didn't have a shrewd business sense to save money for his old age.

A common bond between Leclair and Locatelli was that they both possessed curiosity about the world around them. Locatelli studied birds, church history, political matters, geography, art and even mathematics. Leclair was an educated man, reading Ovid, Virgil, Moliere and Milton.

Who knows what Jean-Pierre Guignon read, or cared about, except maybe getting the concert master's first chair in the King's Concert Spirituel and Royal Orchestra in

1736? Although that sounds like a cheap shot, one must give the man credit, as a great musician; otherwise, he could not have held his own in the musical jousts between Leclair and Guignon in the 1734 concert series. M. Marc Pincherie wrote that there was no clear victory in the battle of the violins. "Their performing styles differed profoundly, Leclair's being more precise, more technically delicate, more cerebral, while Guigon's was more colourful, more fanciful."

The friction between Leclair and Guignon can be understood and forgivable though, in terms of just plain human nature. It's too bad that the one essential ingredient of personality between the two men was missing, i.e., liking each other.

Jean-Pierre Guignon [né Giovanni Pietro Ghignone] Leclair's archrival in the King's court outlived Leclair by another 10 years until January 30, 1774. He was still 15 years shy of the French Revolution. Thankfully, Guignon, the concert master for the King of France, died too early to see the guillotine at work, and that was all for the better!

Jean-Philippe Rameau died a little over half a year later on September 12, 1764, in Paris. This was just over a month before Jean-Marie Leclair met his untimely death at the point of a dagger. The murderer could have at least shown some consideration, and murdered Leclair at a later date, thereby putting some respectable space between the two deaths. Leclair, wherever he was in the heavenly realms, might have felt cheated about Rameau taking away some of his limelight in the close announcements about their deaths.

It is interesting to ask, after all is said and done in one's life, what is the sum total of what they left behind? With some composers, it's the legacy of their manuscripts and what they taught their students. But what is also revealing, is the question of what these men left behind in terms of liquid assets and sellable goods.

First, their legacy. Rameau launched his career into opera with Hippolyte ET Aricie in 1733 when he was 50. Despite an initial stir of criticism, he became a leading composer of French opera, replacing Jean-Baptiste Lully.

In 1746, Leclair went in the same direction with his first operatic work, "Scylla and Glaucus" hoping to change the musical direction of his own life. His work was "politely" received, and his operatic ambitions fizzled out with this first and only operatic work. He went back to composing what he knew best, concertos and sonatas.

Perhaps men of genius are naturally irritable. Rameau was known to be quick to anger and brusque, lacking social graces. In fact, he turned out to be a miser in his old age. He dressed in worn-out clothes, had a single pair of shoes, and played on a dilapidated old harpsichord. One source says that when people went through his rooms after his death, they found a bag of coins, containing 1,691 gold Louis d'or [gold coins].

Jean-Marie Leclair could have used that money to buy a better house in a better part of Paris than the hovel he chose to live in for the rest of his life.

When Locatelli died in March 1764, people in charge of his estate found very valuable items. Collected works of the great Italian maestro Corelli. Paintings by Dutch, Italian and French masters. A collection of instruments and much more which were auctioned off in August 1765, as part of the estate. Who got the money? Did Locatelli's heirs inherit, if he had any, or were debtors paid off? Where is that Ph.D. research student when you need him or her to sort this all out?

It is amazing how many great men of fame blew away their fortune as they got older. Anton Paul Stadler, three

John Hartig   Two Baroque Prodigies

years Mozart's senior, for whom Wolfgang Amadeus Mozart wrote the popular Clarinet Concerto in A, died at the age of 59 of emaciation, which means starvation. After being a Royal Imperial Court Musician from Vienna, one would ask, did the man not have enough money to feed himself at the end of his life? Unless the emaciation was caused by cancer?

Carl Stamitz, violinist and composer, lived through Mozart's lifetime, and had great success in his hometown of Mannheim, not only as a violinist but also as a viola player. He died in poverty in 1801, at the age of 56. There was an auction to pay off the debts he never could pay when he was alive.

Wolfgang Amadeus Mozart, a little boy when Leclair was alive, was buried in a common grave in 1791, though some people refuse to say, "pauper's grave". He was only 35, and one can only guess what the world lost in possible compositions from this musical genius. Where is Mozart's tombstone, so people can honour his gravesite? There is a legend that, in the attempt to find his grave, a gravedigger who apparently knew where the body was buried, snuck the skull out of the grave. Ironically, and despicably so, a similar thing happened to the body of Haydn.

How are the men who have been gifted with musical genius to be treasured during their lifetimes and honoured when they are gone? When they die of emaciation and in abject poverty, should angels not cry?

Jean-Marie Leclair was found dead in the early morning of October 24th, 1764, in the doorway of his little hovel in Paris, stabbed to death! What were his worldly assets? Certainly not his house! The list would include his manuscripts, a broken fiddle, and a hidden bag of money under the mattress. The former landlord, Monsieur Legras, grabbed the loose coins in the bowl that rested on top of the little table by the doorway. That could have been Leclair's drinking money.

Louise Roussel gained access to the house through Monsieur Legras. She confiscated the manuscripts, Leclair's clothes, luckily found the bag of money under the mattress and snagged anything else of value she saw. She even took the broken violin and shattered violin bow, hoping that a repair shop could fix them enough to sell them. She had no idea what a Stradivarius was.

Chapter 24

When it came to the battle of the violins between Jean-Marie Leclair and Jean-Pierre Guignon, it was "a tie" according to one eyewitness in the 1734 concert series. Monsieur Marc Pincherie wrote, "Their performing styles differed profoundly, Leclair's being more precise, more technically delicate, more cerebral, while Guigon's was more colourful, more fanciful."

Probably for this they used a music stand and sheet music. So, how do you choose? Every artist plays in his or her own inimitable way. I'm sure there must have been someone in the audience in 1734 who might say that Jean-Marie Leclair was the clear winner. But then that is an opinion and a matter of taste.

There are so many variables which determine the characteristic of sound and its appeal to the ear. How did the performer feel that day? Grouchy, angry? What is the performer's personality? Buoyant, laid-back? What's the quality of the instrument? A Stradivarius, a $30 fiddle from the pawn shop? The tonality could even come from the dimensions of the player's fingers. How fat or how skinny are the fingers?

Maybe the music itself requires a biting sound, so the player has to follow the specific dynamics written in the piece. Vivaldi's Four Seasons, ranging from Spring's cheery phrasing to Winter's biting staccato. Maybe you, in the audience, don't even like the violin. Maybe your favourite instrument is the flugelhorn, the basset horn or the bassoon. Mozart even wrote a concerto for the bassoon. My second favourite instrument is the oboe, and then the piano.

John Hartig   Two Baroque Prodigies

But speaking about the violin and the types of violins: David Oistrakh started out with a 1702 Conte di Fontana Stradivarius, which he played for 10 years. He switched to a 1705 Marsick Stradivarius. Why? Again, a matter of personal taste. Oistrakh produced a more biting clearer tone with his Marsick Strad. He could put muscles into his notes which carried the sound further out and with a sharper edge than the subdued softness of his 1702 Conte di Fontana Strad. Now, that did not mean he could not produce lyrical and soft sounds with his Marsick when he wanted to.

There is an excellent film written and directed by Bruno Monsaingeon on "The Art of the Violin", Part I and Part II. The film gives you visual and audio recording of the huge range of styles that great players of this and the last century had. They are all good and great players, and it's difficult to say, this one is better than the other one. Commentators include the likes of Ivry Gitlis, Ida Haendel, Hilary Hahn, Laurent Korcia, Yehudi Menuhin, Itzhak Perlman and Mstislav Rostropovitch. We see footage of George Enescu playing "Rumana" No. 3, and Jack Benny quipping with Isaac Stern on stage about the cost of a cheap violin.

Unfortunately, no one will ever be able to hear the real soundtrack of Jean-Marie Leclair, Guignon or Locatelli to compare their quality with modern players. YouTube is wonderful about making recorded video and audio available to the public of our modern virtuosi because someday our current great players, like our 18th century virtuosi, will pass away with the sands of time.

This novella is written as a tribute to the man, Jean-Marie Leclair, who lived from 1697-1764.

Here is a list of my favourite violinists, picked subjectively and haphazardly out of YouTube. When I say that a person's playing is edgy or lyrical, it does not mean that the person could not choose to play in a lyrical style. It depends upon the dynamics required by the piece they are playing, and how the artist chooses to interpret that piece. Edgy or lyrical, the quality of playing is all good and lovely, and I'm glad that we have such musical talents in this world who are able to play at the virtuosic level. Who knows what gave them their gifts or what sacrifices they had to make to develop these gifts, so that they could pass the sound of their gift along to the world?

- 1891-1967 Mischa Elman, precision with emotion, plays Dvorak's "Humoresque", you can hear the little grace notes
- 1901-1987 Jascha Heifetz: sharp biting attacks, crisp and clear, once described as stone-faced with his music, Perlman describes him as a tornado of energy, Heifetz plays Paganini, Caprice No. 24
- 1903-1962 Fritz Kreisler, impeccable rubato depending upon rush of notes or sostenutos, plays "Schön Rosmarin"
- 1916-1999 Yehudi Menuhin, precision like a clock, Menuhin can be accused of standing there like a mechanical automaton, but this is his self-control, Mehuhin plays Paganini, Caprice No. 24
- 1932-1989 Al Cherney, fiddler who played on the Canadian "Tommy Hunter Show", great at double stops, biting style, played "Orange Blossom Special" in Grande Prairie, Alberta circa 1980 when I lived there. My orchestra played the first half, possibly conducted by Kerry Stratton, now a Classical 96.3 FM radio host. Mr. Cherney came in with his suit on a hanger and asked me, "Where's my dressing room?" I said, "I don't know, but the

washroom is over there." He said, "Grande Prairie is a real hick town, isn't it?" I said, "Yes."

- 1945-...Itzhak Perlman, heart wrenching, singing quality, touching the soul, Perlman plays "Raisins and Almonds"
- 1952-...Lenny Solomon, electric violin, known for jazz, biting edge, rhythmic and rocking style, plays "Going to Chicago". I first got introduced to Lenny Solomon's music when I was in my 20s, passed him by at the Mariposa Festival in Toronto. He was wearing a fancy cowboy shirt. I bought his 1974 Myles and Lenny Album, and just loved his violin background music in the song, "Can You Give It All to Me". It would be great to have a time machine to bring Jean-Marie Leclair into the 21st century to square off with Lenny Solomon in a violin joust. Solomon would have to leave his electric violin home though.
- 1956 Nigel Kennedy, aggressive and edgy, great speed and volume contrasts, Kennedy plays Vivaldi's Winter
- 1967 Joshua Bell, emotional and soul rending, Bell plays Ladies in Lavender 2012
- 1976-...James Ehnes, haunting, able to build emotion to disturbing levels, Ehnes plays Sibelius Violin Concerto. James Ehnes is a Canadian, born in Brandon, Manitoba. When I was in fourth year university in 1971, Mark Hymers, Wally Scholtes and I decided to take part of the summer off to drive across Canada to British Columbia. I remember Brandon, Manitoba, particularly, because just outside of the little town, the rear-end housing to my 1963 Pontiac Parisienne cracked, throwing hot gears all over the road. We coasted to

the side of the highway and saw smoke coming out of the wheat field. There were miles and miles of wheat. "Hey, somebody started a fire," I yelled. It was us. We tap danced all over the ditch to get the fire out, then hitch-hiked into Brandon to see if we could find a garage. Yes, they could replace the rear-end housing. It would be a used one from the wrecker's and it would cost $120. I phoned my father, who didn't hesitate to telegram his wayfaring son the money to get us out of this jam. My mother, I'm sure, was listening in, and in her typical European way, was probably saying, "I see black." Needless to say, we got the car fixed by the next day, and drove out of Brandon, Manitoba, not realizing that this little town would be the birthplace of one of the world's greatest violinists, James Ehnes, in 1976. Hitch-hiking was a common practice in our university days. We picked up a hippie, named Milt, in British Columbia who showed us how to use his slingshot to whip stones across the canyon of the Thompson River. To this day, I do not know why I remember his name. Then we picked up a young cowboy who told us he was going to become a famous writer. I can't remember his name. I hope he made it. We ended up taking the ferry to Nanaimo, Vancouver Island, drove across the island, and eventually strolled along the sands of Wreck Beach.

- 1979-...Hilary Hahn, precise with superb volume contrasts, exactitude of clear notes, Hahn plays Mendelssohn Violin Concerto E Minor Opus 64
- 1987-... Nicola Benedetti, full rich sound, singing quality, emotional, great contrasts, plays Erich Korngold's Violin Concerto

John Hartig   Two Baroque Prodigies

I must apologize for the list of unmentioned players, indeed great unmentioned players! There are so many, many virtuosi violinists, who have reached that high stratosphere of excellence! Arthur Grumiaux, Laurent Korcia, Hilary Hahn, Lara St. John, to name a few! I will make it up to them in the next life or maybe the next novel I write!

Chapter 25

Musical Appreciation

My university friends have made me a better person, one who enjoys classical music and the fine arts despite my working-class background. My father was a forklift driver on construction.

Mark Hymers introduced me to Gustav Mahler, and Waldemar Scholtes to choral music. Another friend, Bill Oates, introduced me to Erik Satie. Bill lived at Rochdale College when he attended the University of Toronto in what was then a pretty tough program, MPC, Math, Physics and Chemistry. We went to Sam the Record Man and browsed through all the LPs. I picked up an album of Rimsky-Korsakov's "Scheherazade", played by the London Symphony Orchestra, conducted by Leopold Stokowski. I first fell in love with Rimsky-Korsakov's music when I heard the violin play "The Young Prince and Princess" in an old black and white movie that I was watching on television. I was in grade 8 at the time. Those were the days when I was hooked on Mantovani and also 101 Strings. There was one other record I purchased on sale at Sam the Record Man, and that was Schubert's Unfinished Symphony. I used to set up the portable record player downstairs in the basement, load up my barbells behind a curtain, and then lift weights to the rhythm of Schubert's Unfinished Symphony.

"What are you doing down there?" yelled my mom. "Oh, just listening to music." "Well turn it down!" Which I did, but I kept puffing away at the barbells in a steady rhythm. So, Schubert was good for something, even though he didn't finish the piece. After a workout with those barbells, I myself was finished!

There is sternness in Schubert's Unfinished Symphony which I also find in Beethoven's Fifth. Maybe their breakfast hadn't been cooked right or they needed another cup of coffee, so they were in a grouchy mood when they composed these pieces. Who knows? But there you go, an Unfinished Symphony and a Fifth, both of them rising in anger, then subsiding into a sense of peace, and then flaring up again to throw a challenging fist right into the very face of God.

Mind you, I also fell in line with my peers who also liked Simon and Garfunkel, The Brothers Four, Joan Baez, and Bob Dylan in those days. I like to think of myself as embracing an eclectic taste in music. By 1975 I had "The Best of Spike Jones and his City Slickers" in my record collection, and somehow through about 11 moves, that LP still survived. On the back of Spike's album are little pictures and ads for Perry Como, Al Hirt, Paul Anka, Elvis and Neil Sedaka. Oh yes, there's also an ad for Charley Pride and Henry Mancini Pure Gold...and at the very bottom, you get the call number for Disco-Soul and Polka Variety.

When I was in grade 9, Mr. Frederick Pohl was hired by St. Jerome's High School in Kitchener to teach music in 1962. The school administration had the ambitious idea of creating a high-school orchestra. We heard in the morning announcements that anyone wanting to learn a stringed instrument should come to the Annex across the street after school. I went and picked up my first violin. The school supplied the instruments for free. There was a whole group of us, two bass fiddles, two cellos, one viola and four violins, fresh and eager to become musicians.

Mr. Pohl stopped the rehearsal at one point. He pointed to me, and said, "You just did something clever." I thought I did something wrong and apologized. He said, "Don't be sorry for doing something clever with your fingers." To this day, I don't know what I did, but I appreciated the chance to learn the violin. Mr. Pohl didn't just open the doors for me to violin playing, but he introduced me to Claude Debussy, "Claire de Lune", and other names like Fauré and Ravel.

When I was in grade 11, I took violin lessons from Mr. Voldemars Lasmanis. I remember playing "The Happy Prince" because it was a lyrical and happy piece. I was about grade 6 level at the time, and Mr. Lasmanis told me that The Transylvania Club in Kitchener needed a band to provide the music for their New Year's Eve dance. The band was directed by Professor Walter Scholtes. Professor Scholtes' son Waldemar or Wally played trumpet. He was about my age. Mr. Lasmanis and I were to round out the string section. We each got an envelope with $30 in it at the end of the gig, and I thought, "Hey, there's money in show biz."

I will always have a soft spot in my heart for Mr. Lasmanis. I pedaled my bicycle to his place on Church Street during the winter one year. I was 3 kilometres away from his house, so I had to pedal my Raleigh bicycle from Pandora Ave, down King Street, then up the steep hill on Eby Street, and finally to Mr. Lasmanis' house. Eby Street was a 30-degree steep hill which was a tough climb on my bicycle, especially in winter. It felt like a 90 degree climb by the time I got halfway up the hill. There was snow along the ditch beside the sidewalk.

Half-way up the hill, my violin case popped open. Out fell the towel, and out fell my violin, which slid down the hill like a toboggan. A tree stopped it most unkindly. When

John Hartig Two Baroque Prodigies

I retrieved my violin, the neck was dangling from its dead body. I bundled it up into the case and trudged to the top of the hill and pedaled the rest of the way to Mr. Lasmanis' house for my lesson. I was in tears.

He said, "Well, there will be no Happy Prince this evening." He disappeared to a back room and came out with a bottle of Elmer's Wood Glue. Mr. Lasmanis gently squeezed glue into the crack by the neck, and fitted it tightly in place, not with a rope, but with an electric cord, a brown one, I remember. He said, "Come back next week." There was no charge for that night's lesson. That same violin, a $30 instrument, saw me through the next 9 years.

In 1966, I was in grade 12. The conductor of St. Jerome's High School Orchestra wanted to start a smaller dance band which he picked from the orchestra, musicians who would be willing to play for special events at various Hotels and Inns around the Kitchener-Waterloo area. Mr. Mike Bergauer picked 13 of us and called the group "Opus I". We wore black pants, glitzy green shirts with shiny buttons, and frilly cuffs. I felt silly in the outfit, but hey, we each got $30 after each gig. That was a pretty good return at a time when my violin lessons from Mr. Pohl and then Mr. Lasmanis cost me $5 for one hour. My father was making $2.50 per hour on construction, though he wasn't the one paying for my lessons.

I remember my first pay cheque in grade nine, my first summer on construction working with my dad, hauling in $66 that week, from a special student rate of $1.25 per hour. I think I had to work Saturday. Essentially, I paid for my own lessons.

Later at the University of Waterloo I reached a grade 8 level of playing. I was good enough to be in the orchestra which was put together by Alfred Kunz. But I wasn't good enough when it came to the part which required a quick spiccato. I couldn't keep up, so I just shook my bow furiously. As a result, I would have to say, no, if ever the Toronto Symphony made me an offer, and stick to what I know, playing in amateur orchestras where my fake spiccato is tolerated. Seriously, wherever I've lived, I've always joined a community orchestra and have, I felt, added something positive to the community.

Thinking back on the Leclair assassination, I have never felt envy or hatred toward another player in my orchestra where I wish them harm, like Guillaume-François Vial did with his uncle, Jean-Marie Leclair. I'm just glad I have a healthy hobby. Perhaps, fierce competition rears its ugly head when people actually get close to the top and have an amazing talent and achieve a "super skill". Most likely Vial was quite a good player but not an exceptional phenome, like his uncle. Maybe for that reason, somebody like Locatelli would give lessons only to amateurs and not violinists who were already accomplished. The instinct is primitive, territorial, like a dog guarding his turf. Don't become better than me!

Chapter 26

The Police Investigate

The Lieutenant of Police, Antoine-Gabriel de Sartine, was smoking his pipe. Along with strong taste of Turkish coffee, he enjoyed the whiff of his tobacco. France had been a smoking nation for over two hundred years, already since the New World introduced Europe to this addictive weed. Maybe some of the habit came from watching the tendrils of smoke evaporate into the air like mesmerizing hopes and dreams.

It was a Frenchman, Jean Nicot, who introduced the habit to France in 1560 from Spain. The word, nicotine, is derived from his name. With the stress of his job, de Sartine found his little vices of sipping coffee and smoking tobacco relaxing, a way to cope, and a way to think. Coffee and tobacco put the world into perspective.

Puffing a soft white cloud into the air, de Sartine called his sergeants into his office. "I've found a new clue!" Gentilhomme was ready to take his notepad out. "Not now," said de Sartine, "let me think first."

He explained how he rented a carriage over the past few days, out of the department's budget, to interview several people for whom Jean-Marie Leclair had previously been employed. The "Duc de Gramont" was one of them. "There was no other way to do this, but through the department's expense," he confessed. "Don't write that down yet, Gentilhomme!" he commanded.

A big white puff of smoke came out of his mouth. He paused and tossed back his head. "Now," he nodded to his note taker, "you may write."

"Apparently, Monsieur Leclair was very fond of a certain pocket watch. He showed it to the Duke of Gramont several times and boasted that Louis XV had given the watch to him personally. It was gold plated and had the profile of the King on the inside, as well as the coat of arms. If we find the man with the watch...guess what, Gentilhomme?"

"No, what, Lieutenant?" asked his sergeant.

Lebrusque stepped forward, having no time for Gentilhomme's dull wit, "Why sir, then we have our killer!"

This new clue fired up the investigation. "Thank God for carriages," thought de Sartine, "I'm glad I did not have to walk or go on horse-back. I have enough trouble with my hemorrhoids." Smoking took his mind off the itchiness.

The Lieutenant felt that the list of suspects could be reduced. The gardener was too much of an oaf and did not fit the profile of killer, perhaps petty crimes, but not cold-blooded murder.

The Leclair brothers could also be eliminated because, first of all each of them had success of some sort of their own, and second of all, they all seemed fond of each other as a family.

This left a few possibilities. The 40-year-old nephew, Guillaume-François Vial, who was big and strong, an envious violin player who could not climb to the same heights of success as his uncle, and of course, the ex-wife, Louise Roussel, who apparently was having financial difficulties keeping her engraving business afloat.

The other two possibilities existed as well. A "rôdeur", or prowler, and lastly a mistress or prostitute. De Sartine doubted that a prowler had done the deed. The coins were left in the bowl inside the house. And why would a prowler destroy the violin? Logic dictated that a neighbourhood sneak would have stolen the violin and sold it on the black market. If a prowler had stolen and sold the violin on the black market, then that sort of crime would leave a path of evidence, something which was in the capacity of the police to track down.

> The prostitute? No, she would want hard cash, and would not smash the violin. She would take the coins in the bowl instead. A mistress? Now, that is a possibility which expresses rage and passion. The mistress must not be dismissed.
> The nephew, the ex-wife, the mistress?
> Those were possibilities!

These were things still on the list. De Sartine said to Gentilhomme, "Make a note of that." Gentilhomme said, "Yes, sir."

Other than that, the Lieutenant was hoping to find some bloody clothes perhaps in a side street, and question whose they might be, or better yet, from some drunken wastrel in the tavern to get a confession there. He could not see this happening.

The Lieutenant of Police decided. "Gentlemen, we must find the prostitute and the mistress, so we can strike them off the list."

Gentilhomme asked, "But how do we do that?"

"Use our feet, man. Use our feet!"

They canvassed various streets around the Rue Careme-Prenant.

The streets were narrow and filthy. Shuttered windows pealing and unpainted for years. Clothes lines hanging outside from upper floors. Broken windows blocked by wood. "Les clochards" or unemployed bums sitting on stoops, some of them smoking pipes. Or drinking wine out of the bottle. Where did they get the money to afford these things? Occasionally a man would get up and relieve himself against a building or pee in the street filled with daily garbage, waiting for the rain to flush things away.

The Lieutenant assigned Gentilhomme and Lebrusque to knock on doors on opposite sides of the street and ask if they knew Monsieur Leclair who played the violin. He, himself, took the side streets within a one block radius since he was faster at the job.

They commenced their job late in the morning since nobody in this area seemed to get up early for work. After an hour, Gentilhomme hit pay-dirt.

"Yes," said a sleepy blonde, wiping her eyes and yawning. "He even played his violin for me once, after I serviced him. Didn't like his music, but I knew he was very good at what he did...in both things, I might add, if you know what I mean?"

Gentilhomme said, "I'll be right back with my Lieutenant."

She said, "Is there anything in it for me?" Gentilhomme had to promise her a 10 livre note. She was smart enough to know that paper money had no value, so she held out for a "demi-Louis d'or ", a gold coin worth about 12 livres.

Both Lebrusque and especially de Sartine were impressed with her shrewdness. "Bonjour," she said, "my name is Cloe Bonbon, charmed, I'm sure!" She confided that word had gotten around the neighbourhood that the Monsieur had been killed. "Too bad, he was a nice gentleman, can't say I liked that Baroque stuff, but he paid me regularly after we done."

The policemen thanked her after giving her the "demi-Louis d'or ".

"Now, Lieutenant," she said, sidling up to him with her ample breasts. "For another demi-Louis d'or, the four of us could go upstairs. I've had a 'ménage à trois', but never a 'ménage à quatre'. You could brag to all your friends."

"Mademoiselle Bonbon," declared the Lieutenant, "I'm working. You are attractive and tempting. I want you to know that, but I never mix business with pleasure."

"Shame," she said, "when I'm working, I mix pleasure with pleasure." She laughed. Then she walked around the three officers and touched each one affectionately on the cheek. The Lieutenant she called, Monsieur L'Alpiniste. Gentilhomme, she called, 'Mon petit chou'. Lebrusque, she called 'mon grand lion sans coeur'.

When the three officers got out the door, Lebrusque said quickly, "She sure has our number."
Gentilhomme was more worried about the money they had spent here just on information.
"That's something else out of the police budget," comforted the Lieutenant. "Don't worry about it. I will square it with the chief."

"What do you think Lieutenant?" asked Gentilhomme. "Could she have done it?"

"What do you think, Lebrusque?" asked de Sartine, bouncing the question over to him.

"No," he said, "if she had done it, it would have been like the cottager and his wife who killed the goose that laid the golden egg."

Gentilhomme didn't get it. Lebrusque explained, "She got her living out of Leclair. Why kill him?"

"I was mistaken," thought de Sartine. "About both men. Maybe both of them will go far in the bureaucracy. Gentilhomme for being the 'Yes man' and Lebrusque for getting to the point."

He smiled to himself. "Now all we have to do is find the mistress. I know there is one! Leclair did not suspect the prostitute, Mademoiselle Bonbon. But a regular, steady mistress? That could be a possibility. Leclair had no wife, but he liked routine. He needed a lover with whom he could share his regular time, his feelings, confidences and even his heart."

Chapter 27

Gathering Facts

They canvassed the streets again the next day. Nothing turned up.

"We must refocus our attention," thought the Lieutenant. "Look outside these dirty, dingy streets. What other approach?" He explained to his officers that the prostitute was a dead end. At least, it struck another suspect off the list. The next possibility was to find a steady mistress and hopefully with an interview there, strike her off the list too. The pathway to finding her was clear, at least to him and Lebrusque, not so much to Gentilhomme. "Make a new list," he said to Gentilhomme. "Who were Leclair's friends? His acquaintances? That goes for both Leclair and his ex-wife. We have more canvassing to do, preferably in a better part of town."

They left the seedy streets in the north end of Le Marais, and headed toward the lodgings of a Monsieur Chavagnac, the stone mason in the Rue du Four-Saint-Germain. Certainly, a nicer, more upscale neighbourhood than the Rue de Careme-Prenant, where they had gone door to door earlier in the day and all day yesterday.

When they knocked at the Chavagnac door, a huge burly man opened up, and simply stared at them with unfriendly eyes. He stood there; arms crossed at his chest. "Monsieur Chavagnac?" asked the Lieutenant.

"Yes," growled the huge man. Ah, finally some response out of the tree trunk. "We would like to speak with Louise Roussel. The burly man shouted to the back, "Louise, the police are here." They did not get invited in.

Finally, Louise squeezed in beside the burly giant, and commented, "Ah, the boys in blue. Back again?" The Lieutenant was sure she must have been pretty at some point, perhaps the blue eyes and the dimples. Her face was wrinkled, and the Lieutenant couldn't help but be reminded of an old crow with greedy eyes.

The officers explained from the door that they needed to speak with any other female friends or associates her former husband might have had who could shed light on their investigation. Louise knew what the officers were after, "Ah, a mistress perhaps? Another suspect to add to your list?"

Lieutenant de Sartine was impressed by her quick mind. His eyebrows rose up a bit with new respect for the former Mme 'Leclair'. The Lieutenant held his own council. He thought, "She's a quick one. But maybe there is something she may be willing to divulge, provided she isn't in on Leclair's murder herself. And in that case, she may be sending us on a wild goose chase."

Surprisingly, Louise Roussel was co-operative. She told the police to go back to her old neighbourhood where her engraving shop was, and knock on the door several houses down, the one with the green door. "Ask for Virginie Leblanc. Maybe the whore can tell you something." Then she nodded to Chavagnac, and he squeezed the door shut in the police officers' faces before they could react. It did not make sense trying to knock again. They had, at least, squeezed out a name from the old prune.

If Virginie Leblanc was the mistress, Lieutenant de Sartine found the name ironically ripe with meaning. Virginie meant a freshwater spring and Leblanc meant white, perhaps like the "sins that were washed as white as snow". She had to be the mistress!

"Let's go men," encouraged de Sartine. "We have just enough time to wrap up another fine piece of police work before we go back to the Maréchaussée." Lieutenant de Sartine hailed another carriage for the three of them at the department's expense. The springs of the carriage bounced up and down, and squeaked, as the three men got in and jostled for position.

They were headed for the neighbourhood of the old engraving shop on the Rue Saint-Jacques where they hoped they could find and talk to Virginie Leblanc. The police were making progress with the high hope of wrapping this mystery up with a neat bow and tie. The Superintendent would be pleased.

Lieutenant de Sartine enjoyed surprises. He wondered what was behind the green door as he knocked. A petit lady, about 40, opened the door, and asked, "Can I help you?" She certainly was more attractive than Louise Roussel.

"Are you Virginie Leblanc?" asked the Lieutenant. She nodded.

"It's about Jean-Marie Leclair. He used to live across the street upstairs in the engraving shop. Did you know he was killed?"

"Yes, I heard. Another neighbour told me." It never ceased to amaze the Lieutenant how fast bad news traveled by word of mouth. Maybe it was gossip started by the gardener?

"We'd like to come in and chat," said the Lieutenant.
With all courtesy aside, after a preliminary tea, they talked. Gentilhomme, as usual, took notes and sat to the side.

"Yes, I was his mistress," she openly admitted. She was widowed; her husband having been a carpenter, and a successful one at that, left her a small fortune. She used that to start her own business, a pottery shop, because she had a natural affinity and love, like her husband for making things with her hands. She had a busy and loyal clientele from the nobility in Paris who raved about the glazes, shapes and designs on her plates, bowls, cups and saucers. She even started monogramming them.

"So, it's become a lucrative trade?" asked the Lieutenant.

"Trade, no! It is an art; I am an 'artiste'!" she objected with a spark in her eyes.

"Yes, yes," said the Lieutenant, "I see and appreciate the difference."

She informed the three officers that Jean-Marie Leclair had an eye for pretty women, and so, dropped over some years ago when he was still living with his wife, "just to look at the pottery, you know, at first. Soon it was other things."

"Mind you my husband was dead, and then when Jean-Marie's little dog died, the relationship between him and his wife died too. Things, you might say, 'picked up' between us, however. By then, Jean-Marie had already moved out of Louise's engraving shop and found his own apartment. Our relationship was not only as lovers but as confidantes. Jean-Marie became my friend, and I may add, gentlemen of the police, that I like to consider myself to be more than his mistress."

She confessed she knew Jean-Marie's nature intimately. He could not stay put in one city for very long, and like most men, he was, for want of a better word, "un chien", a dog. The three officers nodded with submissive understanding, and some sympathy.

"I accepted all that in Jean-Marie," she said, "but I did not kill him, if that is what you are here to find out."

Lieutenant de Sartine trusted his instinct. "No, I don't think you killed him. We are sorry for your loss."

"Thank you, I have lost three things in Jean-Marie. A friend, a confidante and a lover."

After the three officers were led outside the green door onto the street again, they hailed another carriage. Amid the jostling and bouncing of their ride, they assessed the interview with the mistress. Gentilhomme could barely keep his pencil from bouncing up and down on the notepad. But he managed.

The Lieutenant commented, "So the mistress is eliminated too from the suspect list. She has enough money of her own. It's not like Leclair was her 'golden goose' and a free meal ticket to an easy life."

He asked, "How many viable suspects does that leave us, Gentilhomme?" Gentilhomme was ready, "The nephew who was ambidextrous, and the ex-wife!" He wrote that down with an exclamation mark in his notepad.

"Let's do some more digging," said the Lieutenant. "We did a good day's work, and tomorrow is another day."

Chapter 28

The moody nephew

Guillaume-François Vial, son of Leclair's younger sister, Françoise, was the most likely suspect. He was big and strong and had a nasty disposition toward others. He had been pestering his uncle for years for a letter of recommendation to the King's court that he was good enough to be a member of the Chapelle and the Chambre du Roy. Leclair thought his nephew did not have any talent of a refined quality. He was a young upstart who thought more of himself than he was. Therefore, Vial was a likely candidate to be the murderer who had means and motive.

When Vial bragged that he was ambidextrous, that revelation pretty well clinched it in de Sartine's mind about Vial being the killer. The way the wounds were inflicted in Jean-Marie Leclair's neck and back, their slant, indicated that the direction of the blow came from the back from a left-handed man. But this was all likelihood and not proof. If there were only some ways to link whatever things Vial touched to the crime scene itself?

But then, Vial probably had visited his uncle on several occasions at the little house, probably begging for some letter of recommendation to a duke or duchess, and any signs of him left there was no proof that he was the one who had wielded the dagger. Strong suspicions were not proof to arrest somebody.

Lieutenant of Police, Antoine-Gabriel de Sartine, complained there was no solid evidence. If only they had the murder weapon itself, perhaps a dagger found hidden in a drawer at the nephew's abode, or if they found that gold pocket watch that reputedly had been presented to

John Hartig   Two Baroque Prodigies

Leclair by Louis XV himself was found on the nephew's person. If only the big brute had a guilty conscience and confessed. Then the case could be solved, neat and tidy, to present to the Superintendent. Glowing promotions would be waiting in the wings for everybody. Maybe Sgt. Gentilhomme might glory in becoming the chief note-taker for the King. The Lieutenant laughed at the idea, and then thought again how frustrated the police were in the case. No proof, no nothing.

The nephew actually did suffer deep pangs of conscience, unknown to anybody. He had insomnia. He took a long walk at about 3:00 or 4:00 in the morning along the Seine River near the Notre Dame Cathedral. The chill and the blackness of the night made his dark thoughts worse.

Yes, he had killed his uncle, stabbed him from behind, three times to make sure. He was so angry he could have strangled his uncle as well. Isn't a blood relative supposed to promote their own? "He said, I was mediocre at best, why should he give me a glowing report?" Vial's blood boiled over at the thought. "Uncle Jean-Marie laughed me in my face." "But Uncle, I am an excellent violinist, a virtuoso, in fact!" "Then show me!" "I faltered on the arpeggios and scratched on my sostenutos." "My boy," said the uncle, "if you practiced more often like I did, then maybe you would get somewhere. Determination and devotion and hours and hours of practice...but then there is also that little thing called, God-given talent." "I'm sure if I got a promotion, was in the right spot, sitting right beside you, Uncle, in the orchestra, the talent would come." "My boy, it does not work that way. You either have it or you don't, and you don't!" "How that hurt; I could have killed him right there and then!"

John Hartig   Two Baroque Prodigies

Guillaume-François Vial had sauntered onto the Pont Neuf Bridge by this time of night in his aimless wandering. He had no real sense of where he was going, except that somehow he found himself on the Pont Neuf. Soon morning would break, but for now, everything was still dark to fit Vial's dark and depressed mood. The Seine River floated leisurely underneath the bridge not caring about the little humans who lived around its banks. The bridge had been started in 1578 and took a quarter of a century to build. It was a beautiful monument, a stone guardian that spanned over Paris' giant water way. How many suicides had the Pont Neuf seen? Vial wondered if he should add himself to that number. He thought seriously about this, as he leaned with his hands clasped over the railing of the bridge.

He wondered what it would take to swim across the Seine. Perhaps he wouldn't make it and drown half-way across. Le Chevalier de Saint-Georges, "the black Mozart", succeeded in a night swim across the Seine River years later prior to the chaos of the French Revolution. Champion fencer and master musician, Saint Georges was the toast of French society and socialized with Marie Antoinette in the 1780s, not only because of his prodigious talents, but also because he was black, exotic and the son of an African slave. During the Revolution, Saint-Georges served as a colonel of the Légion St.-Georges, the first all-black regiment in Europe. The music he composed coincidentally sounded very much like Mozart.

Ironically, Saint-Georges played violin in the "Concert Spirituel" in the early 1770s, cutting a parallel swath like Jean-Marie Leclair some 40 years before. The muscular "mulatto" was appreciated for his flamboyant violin technique, "enrapturing especially the feminine members of the audience."

But Vial did not know any of this as he brooded darkly above the Seine River from the solid safety of the bridge. He wondered how the ripples of the water intersected each other like the lives of people above. Vial gave up the idea of jumping into the river from the bridge, as well as the more ridiculous idea of swimming across the Seine from shore, because he did not have it in him.

Guillaume-François Vial took the dagger deeply tucked into his coat pocket. Looked at it once and heaved it, with his left-hand, as far as he could from the Pont Neuf into the middle of the river. He cried because there was some pinch of regret which now cooled the heat of his old anger toward his uncle. He shook off the soft feeling, and said to himself convincingly, "I'm glad I killed the old bastard anyway."

He then took out the gold pocket watch from the other pocket, opened the case to peer at the image of Louis XV, which he could barely make out by the light of the silvery moon. He felt the engraving more than saw it. He could see the time because of the white face of the watch which made the dials stand out. The time was nearly 5:00 in the morning. He said in a tone, imitating his uncle's voice, "I see by the King's watch, that it is time to get rid of this evidence." He flung the gold pocket watch into the Seine River too as hard as he could. It glittered in the moonlight as it flew in a high arc through the air, fell and then splashed lightly and submerged into the murky depths of the river as if this would hide his sin.

Who was it who said, you cannot step into the same river twice? Yes, Heraclitus, five centuries before Christ, a saying, the simple truth about the universe. The dagger was in the hand of the killer on the night of October 23rd; that same hand played in a church service on the night of

October 24th and moved on now, to throw the evidence into the Seine River.

But Guillaume-François Vial had no interest in the bigger picture of life or the universe. He was focused on his own petty acts of the moment, and how to get rid of the dagger, which would link him to the killing. He got the idea to get rid of the evidence of the dagger and pocket watch luckily before the police thought of looking for them either on his person or at his lodging.

"Now that this is done," said Vial to himself, "I can go home and sleep soundly."

"No pangs of conscience and no regrets," he vowed.

Chapter 29

Means, Motive, Opportunity

"If only we had the dagger and the pocket watch," thought Lieutenant de Sartine. "It would serve justice if we could catch the nephew with those items in his house. We'd have him red-handed."

Then a thought occurred to him. "What if he's thrown them into the Seine River?" He asked Sgt. Lebrusque to be discreet and to follow the nephew, just in case he took a walk toward the river. Lebrusque and Gentilhomme could take turns in a stakeout at the apartment. "Wherever he goes, you go, understand? But do it at a distance and try not to be too obvious."

The only problem was the police came up with their idea too late. Vial had already disposed of the dagger and the pocket watch several nights earlier. He was not greedy enough to keep his uncle's gold-plated watch. He thought of it as a trophy at first, but then thought better of it, as a silly idea. In fact, he grew to hate the sight of the watch. He also knew it was a stupid idea to keep the dagger in his apartment.

De Sartine, meanwhile, was hoping that Vial was one of those killers who kept a trophy of his kill, but apparently, he wasn't.

The Lieutenant tried to put himself into the mind of the killer. "You'd think the gold pocket watch was too tempting to just throw away, but then if the watch reminded him too much of his late uncle, then where would he dispose of it?"

"If I were the killer," said the Lieutenant to himself, "I'd throw both items into the river. Yes, that is what I would do. And if Vial was successful in doing that, then Vial is a fish that unfortunately got away. The Superintendent won't be pleased."

After several days, both Gentilhomme and Lebrusque reported that Vial wasn't going near the river, but that he frequented the tavern instead, *La Dame Chantante,* like usual. He played billiards there, drank his wine and then went home, apparently straight-off to bed. He brought no prostitute home with him and apparently had no mistress. "Maybe he's not well liked," quipped Gentilhomme. "Or else, he smells," commented Lebrusque. They had no good words to say about Guillaume-Francois Vial.

The Lieutenant leaned back in his chair, and puffed smoke thoughtfully from on his pipe, "If he went to the river before we came up with our brilliant idea to follow him, then he was one step ahead of us. If the dagger and pocket watch are already at the bottom of the river, we don't stand a chance of finding them." He consoled his sergeants, saying, "and that gentlemen, is something beyond our control. How about if we knock off for the night?"

Thus, timing and luck conspired to give the killer a break. The Lieutenant had said at the beginning of the investigation, "We may never know who the killer is." Now at the end, they did know who the killer was, but they could do nothing about it, nor put it in the official record.

Unknown to the three police officers, they almost caught a break three years later in 1767. Guillaume-François Vial requested that Louise Roussel set up a "business meeting" with him at the engraving shop. Vial wanted a booklet he had written to be published. It wasn't much, 6 pages, entitled, "L'arbre généalogique de l'harmonie". The title of the pamphlet seemed longer than the actual tract. Compared to the beauty, originality and importance of musical compositions and works of art, which passed through the shop over the years, Vial's little pamphlet was shallow, small and of no real importance. He just wanted it published because he wanted to be published, so he could claim he was an actual published author.

A long title for 6 pages! Ludicrous! Louise laughed at him. "If you do not publish it," he threatened, I will go to the police and explain how you paid me to murder my uncle, your ex-husband." Louise gave in; she bought his continued silence by publishing the little tract, "L'arbre généalogique de l'harmonie". The long-winded title made him sound so important and "erudite". But often with people who have a higher opinion of themselves than they actually are, are long-winded in speeches and phrases padded with florid words to cover up that there is really nothing under their "erudite" exterior.

Louise was 64 years of age at the time of her husband's death. Vial was 40 years old. Louise was old enough to worry about money in her old age; who would provide for her? Vial was old enough to hate his uncle for not promoting a career that could have soared!

Louis Roussel was proud of her engraving business which she inherited from her father. It was a rare thing for a woman in the 18th century to own her own business and to run it by herself. However, when her ex-husband died in 1764, she found debts which were catching up with her. His death was like a Godsend, giving her access to his remaining assets in manuscripts, some coins, clothes and even the broken violin, which she could sell. She had a new infusion of cash in her engraving business.

She swooped in on the old house, collected his belongings and auctioned them off. She reissued his compositions, and then took a couple of as yet unpublished manuscripts to her shop, so she could publish and print them. She salvaged his unpublished manuscripts, not as a good deed to save his works for posterity, but because there was money to be had in republishing to save her shop.

The nephew did not show up for the funeral on October 25th at the Eglise Saint-Laurent. Louise made sure she was there; however, as well as at a later memorial service, held at the Eglise de Feuillants in the Rue Saint-Honoré on December 2nd, 1765. The "Concert Spirituel" saw to it that both its choir and orchestra performed Mondonville's "De Profundis" during that memorial service. It was truly a moving ceremony in remembrance of a great violinist and composer.

The three police officers thought they might as well show up at the 1765 Concert Spirituel's commemoration, in hopes of cornering the nephew, and perhaps having another chat with him in which he might let something slip. But since he did not show up, they had to sit and enjoy the music, somewhat to Lebrusque and Gentilhomme's consternation.

Louise Roussel died in 1774. Guillaume-François Vial continued to live a life of insignificance, with no obvious documentation about the date of his death. Neither one of them was ever charged or arrested for the murder of Jean-Marie Leclair. The case remained unsolved, despite strong suspicions. They also remained insignificant in the annals of history.

Jean-Marie Leclair received belated accolades for his mastery of music. He has been called "the French Bach" and "the French Corelli". It is said that he did not like extra flourishes in his music, just for the sake of ornamentation. He preferred a direct simple approach in his compositions. The man was knowledgeable both in the solo instrument for which he composed, as well as the well-balanced sense of harmony in a symphony. He loathed fawning and flattery. Jean-Marie Leclair is recognized as the founder of the French school of violin. He left quite a legacy, and possibly could have added more had he not been murdered so cowardly, as to be stabbed from behind in late October 1764.

*****

Musicians are generally acknowledged to be nice people because, well, because they are given a special gift by God. They are also generally considered to be sensitive people with a keen appreciation of the arts. Maybe there's a warning too that there is a Dr. Jekyll and Mr. Hyde in all of us because the nephew, a violinist, killed his uncle, a better violinist.

There is a profound piece of irony in Leopold Mozart's letter to his son, a piece of advice he wanted to impart to his young son, Wolfgang, who was 22 years of age at the time. This letter was penned 14 years after Jean-Marie Leclair met his untimely death. Father Leopold recalls that, in his own youth, "I avoided all contact with others and in particular preferred not to become over familiar with people of our own profession." In other words, he tells his son to stay away from musicians! Though Leopold Mozart was serious, to us the thought of such advice from a musician father to his musician son is ironically amusing.

Time is no friend to no man. Other cases kept piling up on Lieutenant de Sardine's desk. Leclair's file was shuffled off to the side into the cold case file, UNSOLVED, NO ARRESTS. Lebrusque and Gentilhomme were assigned to other duties. Soon, the file of Jean-Marie Leclair was dumped into the bottom drawer of Lieutenant de Sardine's desk.

While Leclair lay dead in his grave, the world continued with its own concerns and its own inevitable direction. Throughout the 18th century the French government was not able to control its mounting debts. It was the common folk, the average taxpayers, who were obliged to pay for "a war badly begun [the War of the Austrian Succession 1741-1748] and badly supported, the greed of a prime minister, of a mistress, of foolish expenditures, and the prodigality of the King."

This all ruined the finances of France, with the last straw coming when Louis XVI dismissed his finance minister, the Swiss-born, Jacques Necker. Paris was in a direct path toward the French Revolution in 1789.

John Hartig   Two Baroque Prodigies

Postface

Unfortunately, what I dug up about Lean-Marie Leclair has been a paucity of facts and little summaries, yielding mainly a string of dates, locations and what he did in certain places at certain times. A skeletal structure of the barest documentation! Certainly, not enough to fill a detailed biography of one of the greatest violinists of the 18th century France! Jean-Marie Leclair was no minor character in musical history. He established the French school of violin. He was dubbed "the French Corelli" and "the French Bach".

As an author, I asked what one can do with only a skeletal string of dates and locations. As a writer, I decided that I needed to fill in that skeletal framework with enough fancy and catchy dialogue to generate a novel, or at least a "novelette". I think I've succeeded, and I hope you enjoy this story of fact mixed with fiction.

Jean-Marie Leclair was one of 8 children, the oldest born in 1697. His parents owned a haberdashery business. His father played cello as a hobby; the mother made gowns for ladies of the nobility. Jean-Marie made his living at first as a ballet dancer, and then concentrated on his talent as violinist and composer. When he took advanced studies with accomplished violin player, Giovanni Battista Somis, he was advised to shove his ballet dancing into the background and make the violin his primary occupation. That advice served him well because Jean-Marie Leclair gained a reputation as a great musician.

Later in life, he deliberately chose to live in a seedy part of Paris. We know that he was stabbed to death outside his home at the age of 67, cruelly murdered, and the crime was never solved.

This novella is mostly made-up. Historians, I'm sure, will find inaccuracies in the factual parts of my work. However, this small novel is meant to entertain and not to be accurate as a full-proof biography. I must admit that my research and making up the ensuing imagined part of Jean-Marie's secret life has been fun, mixing fact with fiction. It has also been quite instructive digging up facts about the lifestyles, the clothes, the homes, the mores and even the foods of the 18th century in France.

Resources and References
JEAN-MARIE LECLAIR 1697-1764

BIOGRAPHY AND MURDER

Leclair violin owner, Italian conductor Guido Rimonda
https://www.bizzarrobazar.com/en/2018/02/27/le-violon-noir/

Jean-Marie Leclair – Wikipedia
https://en.wikipedia.org/wiki/Jean-Marie_Leclair

Jean – Marie Leclair (1697 – 1764) - early-music.com
http://www.early-music.com/what-is-early-music/jean-marie-leclair-1697-1764/

Jean-Marie Leclair Biography
https://play.primephonic.com/artist/jean-marie-leclair-1697

Who murdered Jean-Marie Leclair- - Orchestra of the Age of Enlightenment
http://www.oae.co.uk/murdered-jean-marie-leclair/

What Killed the Great and Not So Great Composers? Joseph W. Lewis, Jr., M.D., Google Books
https://books.google.ca/books?id=Jf5LiICDWl8C

Une mort trop petite pour eux (2-10) - Actualités - Ôlyrix
https://www.olyrix.com/articles/olyrix/156/une-mort-trop-petite-pour-eux-610

John Hartig   Two Baroque Prodigies

Rebels and Rivalries - SFEMS
http://sfems.org/?p=8085

Murder in the Rue Careme-Prenant
http://www.interlude.hk/front/jean-marie-leclair/

Finale Marked Presto- The Killing of Leclair on JSTOR
https://www.jstor.org/stable/948121?seq=1#page_scan_tab_contents

A Baroque Music History Murder Mystery - Music History Matters
https://musichistorymatters.org/juicy-baroque-murder-mystery/

Jean-Marie Leclair pdf
https://www.wrightmusic.net/pdfs/jean-marie-leclair.pdf

Jean-Marie Leclair - Biography & History - AllMusic
https://www.allmusic.com/artist/jean-marie-leclair-mn0001439658/biography

Jean-Marie Leclair (1697-1764)
https://www.musicologie.org/Biographies/l/leclair_jean_marie.html

Jean-Marie Leclair (1697-1764) - Find a Grave Memorial
https://www.findagrave.com/memorial/21793061/jean-marie-leclair

Jean-Marie Leclair- Seduction and Rococo Art - Playing the Palace https://www.artsjournal.com/palace/2013/06/jean-marie-leclair-seduction-and-rococo-art.html

Jean-Marie Leclair, a Narrative of His Life and Death - YouTube
https://www.youtube.com/watch?v=HLaLBQ5xegs

The Leclair Caper – Simanaitis Says
https://simanaitissays.com/2018/02/01/the-leclair-caper/

L'assassinat de Jean-Marie Leclair- Une des plus grandes énigmes criminelles du XVIIIe siècle eBook- Gérard Gefen, Philippe Beaussant, Roger Le Taillanter- Amazon.fr- Amazon Media EU S.à r.l-
https://www.amazon.fr/Lassassinat-Jean-Marie-Leclair-grandes-criminelles-ebook/dp/B077NHG3HN

Jean-Pierre Guignon, *né* Giovanni Pietro Ghignone (10 February 1702 – 30 January 1774) was an 18th-century Franco-Italian composer and violinist
https://en.wikipedia.org/wiki/Jean-Pierre_Guignon/

THEIR MUSIC

Women & Music - A History -Google Books
https://books.google.ca/books?id=XBXggAcjnEoC

The Birth of French Opera
https://en.wikipedia.org/wiki/French_opera#The_birth_of_French_opera:_Lully

Dances of the Baroque Era
https://socialdance.stanford.edu/Syllabi/baroque.htm

18TH CENTURY PARIS

A Concise History of FRANCE, Second Edition, Roger Price, Cambridge University Press, 2005 pp. 87-89

Louis The Beloved: The Life of Louis XV, Olivier Bernier, Doubleday 1984.

Queen of Fashion: Marie Antoinette, Caroline Weber, Henry Holt & Co. 2006.

Paris in the 18th century
https://en.wikipedia.org/wiki/Paris_in_the_18th_century#Food_and_drink

Paris in the 18th century
https://en.wikipedia.org/wiki/Paris_in_the_18th_century#Workers,_servants_and_the_poor

The Paris Police
https://en.wikipedia.org/wiki/Paris_in_the_18th_century

The 18th century social sciences McMaster pdf
https://socialsciences.mcmaster.ca/econ/ugcm/3ll3/see/18thCentury.pdf

NEWS AND COFFEE

HISTORY OF THE EARLY PARISIAN COFFEE HOUSES
http://www.web-books.com/Classics/ON/B0/B701/16MB701.html

English coffeehouses in the 17th and 18th centuries - Wikipedia
https://en.wikipedia.org/wiki/English_coffeehouses_in_the_17th_and_18th_centuries

18th century coffee houses.docx
http://www.web-books.com/Classics/ON/B0/B701/16MB701.html

17th century - How did people receive news before the advent of the newspaper- - History Stack Exchange
https://history.stackexchange.com/questions/1976/how-did-people-receive-news-before-the-advent-of-the-newspaper

A Brief History of the First French Encyclopedia - Mental Floss
http://mentalfloss.com/article/502589/brief-history-first-french-encyclopedia

HOW THEY LIVED

Hygiene In The 18th Century – YouTube
https://www.youtube.com/watch?v=BoT3C-ae8io

A brief history of body odor
https://theweek.com/articles/614722/brief-history-body-odor

Madame Isis' Toilette- Keeping clean in the 18th century
http://madameisistoilette.blogspot.com/2014/09/keeping-clean-in-18th-century.html

10 Revolting Facts About the 18th Century - List verse
https://listverse.com/2012/10/22/10-revolting-facts-about-the-18th-century/

A quick history of domestic lighting - Lucy Worsley
http://www.lucyworsley.com/a-quick-history-of-domestic-lighting/

keeping warm in the 18th century - Jane Austen's World
https://janeaustensworld.wordpress.com/tag/keeping-warm-in-the-18th-century/

Heating the 18th century house
https://www.jstor.org/stable/988150?seq=1#page_scan_tab_contents

18th Century Marriage Customs
http://www.wondersandmarvels.com/2014/07/18th-century-marriage-customs.html
Late 1800s Wedding
https://www.geriwalton.com/marriage-etiquette-france-late-1800s/

The Composers' Houses
by Gerard Geffen in French,
no trans. , could not get a copy

CONTEMPORARIES

Jean-Pierre Guignon - Wikipedia
https://en.wikipedia.org/wiki/Jean-Pierre_Guignon

John Hartig   Two Baroque Prodigies

Joseph Haydn - Wikipedia
https://en.wikipedia.org/wiki/Joseph_Haydn

Symphony No. 22 (Haydn) - Wikipedia
https://en.wikipedia.org/wiki/Symphony_No._22_(Haydn)

The Mozarts in London – Music Blog
https://blogs.bl.uk/music/2018/05/mozartinlondon.html

Leopold Mozart's Advice to His Son Wolfgang Amadeus - The Intermediate Period
https://theintermediateperiod.wordpress.com/2015/09/20/leopold-mozarts-advice-to-his-son-wolfgang-amadeus/

European Mozart ways - European Mozart ways
https://www.mozartways.com/content.php?m=2

Visit from the child Mozart, 1763-1764 – Palace of Versailles
http://en.chateauversailles.fr/discover/history/key-dates/visit-child-mozart-1763-1764

Jean-Baptiste Lully
Music, style and influence
https://en.wikipedia.org/wiki/Jean-Baptiste_Lully - Ballets_de_cour

Acknowledgements

When I first started out as a novelist, I forgot to mention Acknowledgements. Now, I realize that it is important to publicly thank people because people need to feel appreciated.

Thanks to my high-school English teacher, Mr. William Klos, who ignited a love of literature in me during my formative literary years.

When I was 41, I had open-heart surgery to replace a crusted aortic valve. It had been degenerating for years, I assume from the rheumatic fever I suffered in the refugee camp in Austria as a baby shortly after World War II. In 1985, the damage caught up with me. I could not walk up stairs without huffing and puffing, nor walk a city block without vomiting. It looked like I would be dead within the year.

I want to thank Dr. Barwynski, a heart surgeon, at St. Boniface Hospital in Winnipeg, who gave me a St. Jude Valve, size 23, which has gifted me with an additional 37 years of life, during which time I got married and have written some 20 odd books.

Dr. Barwynski, squeezed me in on a Sunday for my heart surgery using Canada's Universal Healthcare System, which made it possible for me not to go into a debt which could have taken me years to pay off. If only, the rest of the world would take care of its citizens that way then the world might be a better place.

Diethard Schuender, my dear friend, is my spell-check when the computer misses something. He also points out inconsistencies in my writing which I must correct and any other glaring mistakes which I must fix up. Diet is a reliable friend and an invaluable editor and proofreader. I told Diet, one time, that writing a novel was like gardening; you have to keep up with the weeding to get it right.

I'd like to thank Lubo Cekota who is not shy about giving his opinions about history and pointing out inconsistencies. Dates and the facts have to be right.

Veronika Reiser, at the Rittenhouse Public Library, in Vineland dug up some excellent resources for me about France and how people lived in the 18th century. That was for the Jean-Marie Leclair murder mystery of 1764.

Helen Basson, former wardrobe mistress at the Stratford Shakespearean Festival, shared knowledge about how unsanitary it was to walk on the seedy streets of cities in the 18th century for ladies wanting to protect the fringes of their long dresses.

Thanks to my wife, Marjorie, who prefers to remain anonymous and who let me sneak off at midnight, close the bedroom door, and fire up the computer with a cup of tea by my side, so I can type. Insomnia has its good points.

****

John Hartig   Two Baroque Prodigies

Publication Contributions:
by John Hartig

1. Poem by John Hartig p. 43, "I Walked to Kenny's Grave Today", <u>Solitude: A Collection of New Canadian Poetry</u>, publ. 2009, Polar Expressions Publishing, Maple Ridge, BC.

2. Poem by John Hartig, "Songs of Innocence and Experience", <u>The Journey: A Collection of New Canadian Poetry</u>, publ. 20010, Polar Expressions Publishing, Maple Ridge, BC.

3. Short story by John Hartig, "Coffee Break", <u>Formation: New Canadian Short Stories</u>, publ. 2010, Polar Expressions Publishing, Maple Ridge, BC.

4. Short story by John Hartig, "Courage Getting Old", <u>From Across the River</u>, publ. 2011, Poetry Institute of Canada, Victoria B.C.

5. Center Page Photo Spread: <u>Our Canada – A Country for All Seasons</u>, "Spring Blossoms in Niagara-on-the-Lake," publ. 2012

6. Photo Design Ad Published: ARABELLA, Magazine Publication of Canadian Art, Architecture and Design, "Spring Awakenings 2012 Edition", Full page photo ad for *Granny's Boot Antiques* in Vineland, "Unique Folk-Art, Vibrant and Alive!" John Hartig Photos.

Books
Fiction
The New Crusades, John Hartig, second ed. 2021, first publ. 2015, by Tellwell, under my penname, Waldemar Guenter, avail. through Amazon and Ingram
The New Crusades: The Sequel, John Hartig, second ed. 2021, first publ. by Friesen Press, 2016, under my pennames of Waldemar Guenter and Alexander Kucharski, avail. through Amazon and Ingram
Duplicity, publ. Amazon, 2018, John Hartig. avail. through Amazon and Ingram
Who Killed Jean-Marie Leclair? A Baroque Murder Mystery, publ. Amazon, 2019, John Hartig. avail. through Amazon and Ingram
Love and Faith Trilogy, Books I, II, III, publ. Amazon, 2019, John Hartig. avail. through Amazon and Ingram
The Polish Cowboy, publ. Amazon, 2019, John Hartig. avail. through Amazon and Ingram
The Tipperary Kid, publ. Amazon, 2019, John Hartig. avail. through Amazon and Ingram
John's Shorts: Little Stories with Big Ideas, publ. Amazon, 2022, John Hartig. avail. through Amazon and Ingram
John's Hidden Gems: Short Story Collection, publ. Amazon, 2022, John Hartig. avail. through Amazon and Ingram
Things Have Gotta Get Better Than This, publ. Amazon, 2022, John Hartig. avail. through Amazon and Ingram
The Chosen: A Violin Story, publ. Amazon, 2022, John Hartig. avail. through Amazon and Ingram
Jonah's Journey, publ. Amazon, 2022, John Hartig. avail. through Amazon and Ingram.
Johann Joachim Quantz, Gift of the Flute, publ. 2022, John Hartig, avail. through Amazon and Ingram.

John Hartig   Two Baroque Prodigies

The Sasquatch, Book 1, publ. 2023, John Hartig, avail. through Amazon and Barnes and Noble.

The Sasquatch: The Sequel, publ. 2023, John Hartig, avail. through Amazon and Barnes and Noble.

The Sasquatch Family: Volume 1 Human Greed and Volume 2, Redemption. Available through Amazon. 2024 John Hartig, copyright.

Non-Fiction

<u>Time in a Bottle Trilogy</u>, Books I, II, III, publ. Amazon, 2019, John Hartig. avail. through Amazon and Ingram
<u>You Love Our Milk and Honey</u>, Book I, II, publ. Amazon, 2020, John Hartig. avail. through Amazon and Ingram
<u>The Second Wave: Living Through Trump and Covid</u>, publ. Amazon, 2021, John Hartig. avail. through Amazon and Ingram.
<u>77 Looking Back: My Sort of Diary 2022-2023</u>, publ. Amazon, 2023, John Hartig,

Other

Can You Imagine? A children's picture book with poetry, publ. Amazon, 2019, John Hartig. avail. through Amazon and Ingram
Poetry Like Raindrops, publ. Amazon, 2019, John Hartig. avail. through Amazon and Ingram
Battle of the Violins, publ. Amazon, 2019, John Hartig. avail. through Amazon and Ingram
John's Photobook Series, Ball's Falls to Niagara Falls, publ. Amazon, 2021, John Hartig Photos. avail. through Amazon and Ingram
Louis Riel and Me, publ. Amazon, 2021, John Hartig, a historical fiction. avail. through Amazon and Ingram
Give Us Hopes and Dreams, publ. Amazon, 2021, John Hartig. avail. through Amazon and Ingram
Where Do Good Atheists Go? publ. Amazon, 2021, John Hartig. avail. through Amazon and Ingram
We Are Not Alone: Civilizations in Outer Space publ. Amazon, 2022, John Hartig. avail. through Amazon and Ingram.
The Cosmos: Origins and Aliens, publ. Amazon, 2022, John Hartig. avail. through Amazon and Ingram.
Johann Joachim Quantz, publ. Amazon, 2022, John Hartig, avail. through Amazon.
Two Baroque Prodigies, "Quantz flute tutor for Frederick the Great, Leclair, violinist murdered in 1764", publ. Amazon, 2022, John Hartig, avail. through Amazon.

*****

John Hartig   Two Baroque Prodigies

John's Photobook Series

Who knows what Photobook is next? The possibilities are limited only by the imagination! avail. through Amazon and Ingram

Photobooks are 8.5x8.5"

The Bruce Trail

The Niagara Peninsula

Ball's Falls

John Hartig   Two Baroque Prodigies
Port Dalhousie

The War of 1812

Sights in the
Niagara Peninsula

Granny's Boot Antiques

Niagara-on-the-Lake

Morningstar Mill

Niagara Falls

5 Waterfalls in Niagara

John Hartig — Two Baroque Prodigies

Fair Havens 70th Anniversary

Two of my Favourite Seasons

From The Bottom Up

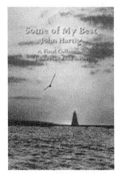

Some of My Best

My Choicest Picks 1

*****

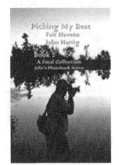

My Choicest Picks 2

John Hartig   Two Baroque Prodigies

- John Hartig Novels through Amazon and Ingram, google title and John Hartig
- John's Photobook Series ordered directly from Amazon and Ingram.
- Prints, any size enlargements, e-mail John directly to place an order. Pickup at the house, otherwise + shipping cost

John Hartig

John lives in Ontario. Photobooks and prints are available for home or office.

CONTACT
johnehartig@gmail.com
johnhartig.ca
Or just Google
John Hartig
Photography

Made in the USA
Monee, IL
09 February 2025

10913031R10164